Hakim Bey

Real and Unreal

Th. Metzger

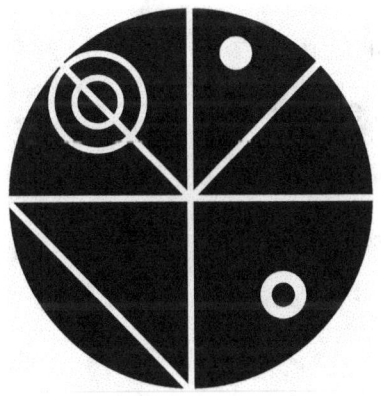

mogtus-sanlux
Columbus Indiana 2023

Hakim Bey: Real and Unreal by Th. Metzger
Copyright © 2023 Th. Metzger
All rights reserved.

Select Bibliographies by Trevor Blake
Copyright © 2023 Trevor Blake
All rights reserved.

Cover Design by Kevin I. Slaughter.

Proofreading by Teresa Bergen.

mogtus-sanlux 305
~mogtus-sanlux
mogtus-sanlux.one

Metzger, Th.
[English]
Hakim Bey: Real and Unreal
ISBN 978-1-944651-27-5 (paperback)
ISBN 978-1-944651-31-2 (hardback)
1. Literature
2. Biography
Th. Metzger
Peter Lamborn Wilson / Hakim Bey (1945 - 2022)

127 House: At every turn in its thought society will find us — waiting.

Advance Praise for
Hakim Bey: Real and Unreal
by Th. Metzger

Bob Fingerman, cartoonist / author (*Minimum Wage*; *Pariah*)
For decades I've referred to Th. Metzger as "the most interesting person I know." And while that remains true, I now have a deeper understanding of his origin story, at the toner-smudged tutelage of his be-fezzed mystique madman mentor. This book is a grand piece of backwards-glancing at small press culture and one of its most prolific fonts of esoterica, the inestimable Hakim Bey.

Steve Sherrill (*The Minotaur Takes a Cigarette Break*)
Th. Metzger navigates narratives and realities (and unrealities) of all sorts here, with both fine finesse and the delicacy of a bulldozer. An ecstatic bulldozer. Is it biography? Autobiography? Or maybe a fiery jig or fling or fancy-dance through all sorts of cultural landscapes, earthbound and otherwise. Where does Hakim Bey stop and Metzger begin? Doesn't matter. What it is, is a good read.

Erik Davis (*TechGnosis* and *High Weirdness*)
This account filled in so many questions and lacunae, and pumped up my own imaginings with more remarkable imaginings. I loved how NY folklore got woven in, all this great arcana.

Derek Owens (*The Villagers* and *Memory's Wake*)
We can count on one hand the rarefied few who truly knew the effervescent Hakim Bey well enough to write an authentic *biographique* of the infamous unholy man. Th. Metzger is the opposable thumb on that hand. Only a fez-sporting late century Moor, an Old Weird New Luddite, a *sui generis* scholar of crypto-religious kitsch-funk could offer up this manic account of the "man made out of words, a story telling itself." To be sure this effulgent, hallucinatory deep dive into Bey's, and Metzger's, friendship offers insights into the mind and world of this trickster magus — but more than that it's one sweet portrait of two singular thinkers, their mutual love and admiration for each other.

Contents

Hakim Bey: Real and Unreal

Send Whatever You Can 1
Zines 5
Initiation 11
Back from the Shadows 17
The Prophet 21
Moorish Mail-Order Mysticism .. 27
Chaos 33
Poetic Facts 41
True Desires 45
Seventeen Messengers 49
The Astral Convention 53
The Prophet Says Wear Your Fez to the TAZ 59
TAZ 69
Pirates 73
Luddites 79
Visitations 85
Time Off 93
Apocrypha 97
Anarcho-Monarchism 103
Lost / Found 107
Alchemy of the Word 111
Ganesh Baba 117

Boundary Violations 121
MOR 127
Dear Th. (1) 133
Grand Metropolitan 135
Cartographic Mystery 139
The Grange 147
Comics 151
The Gifts of the Fezzi 155
Snakes and Ladders 159
Dear Th. (2) 163
Meet the Moors 167
Stay Irrational 171
Dr. Omar 175
"The Dog" and Islam 179
The Sorcerers 181
Big Pink and Boleskine House 189
Angelican Voodoo 195
Pang Yang and Penn Yan 199
Madness and Escape 205
The Hidden 209
Back to the Caves 213
Penn Yan and Pang Yang 219

Addendum

Select Bibliography Hakim Bey 227
Select Bibliography Th. Metzger 233

Hakim Bey

wa salaam

Real and Unreal

SEND WHATEVER YOU CAN

We want to be amazed.
That's how it all began. Amazed and awakened.
Another phrase whispered from the page to my inner ear: *the gratification of almost-unheard-of desires.* This was both seduction and summons, a breathless Call to the Wild. I had no idea who these people were, nor what they really wanted. Their flyer had materialized in my mailbox, clamoring for me to send back unidentifiable texts and sheer self-abandoned craziness.

Only later did I closely inspect the postage stamp: featuring a wooden duck head, part of a Folk Art USA series. A tiny picture of a hunter's decoy hand-carved a hundred years ago, converted into currency (22 cents), and spit-glued to the envelope.

Inside, I found a different kind of lure, an enticement for submissions to something calling itself *Semiotext(e) USA*. The flyer had been banged out on a manual typewriter and cheaply xeroxed, the text covering most of both sides of the page: skewed and passionate, veering from solicitation to screed. The editors' desire was to create an overflowing collection of sermons, rants, broadsheets, pamphlets, manifestos, and psychotopography. Their fervid dream: an anthology that would provide charts of energies, a secret map of the USA leading the reader to unnamed hidden places.

Gazing down the first side of the flyer, I was already snagged. Flipping it over I saw that one of the editors had added a handwritten note, dated April 1, 1985: *I loved your poems in Seditious Delicious. Send whatever you can.* I didn't, at the time, notice that his solicitation had been written on All Fools Day.

So, a strange somebody had read "Saw Tooth" (my tribute to alto sax genius Eric Dolphy, Dadaism in Berlin, and the abrasive cleansing power of dirt.) Had it indeed appeared in *Seditious Delicious,* or in another homemade zine with only a few dozen readers? I wasn't sure. Whatever the case, someone in a misty somewhere had loved my poem, and reached out via the U.S. Mail to pull in more of my work.

Until then, my mailbox had been purely functional – a place where ordinary bills, crap ads, and occasional banal vacation postcards appeared. After receiving this appeal, and sending in reply "Black Wax" and "X-Axis Versus Jocko," the postal system started to mutate, becoming over-fecund, seething with possibilities.

At the same bookstore where I eventually found the finished *Semiotext(e) USA,* I was caught by *High Weirdness by Mail — a Directory of the Fringe.* It mocked and praised (sometimes simultaneously) hundreds of mad prophets, crackpots, kooks and true visionaries, whose private publications flew well below pop culture radar. I bought a roll of a hundred stamps and began sending my queries, with The Usual (that is: a dollar bill or a stamped, self-addressed envelope), into the Great Unknown.

ZINES

Semiotext(e) USA contained writings by such high-hip luminaries as William Burroughs, Rudy Rucker, Jean Baudrillard, and Allen Ginsberg. However, most of the 350 pages were filled with bizarre detritus from the real fringes of the American literary underground. This was at the peak of the zine phenomenon, when thousands of handmade, xeroxed publications were slithering back and forth through the U.S. Mail. The Feds had no inkling how much High Weirdness they were delivering every day, and if any postal inspector had looked closely, there would have been investigations, if not arrests. At the back of the *USA* anthology was a motley collection of personal ads. Most were fake, or poetically-contrived, filthy haikus scrawled on an imaginary bathroom wall. And they included contact info, i.e. old fashioned mailing addresses.

I rented a U.S. Post Office box and created a quasi-fictitious identity: Ziggurat. My box was soon stuffed with madness from distant places. Before being destroyed by the internet, zines were the best way for poetical ranters, egoists, anarchists, audio-cassette pirates, punk rock fanatics, collage artists, cosmic drug brothers, purveyors of homemade porn, self-righteous vegans, and lone-nut scholars to disseminate their work. To keep my box from overflowing, I had to stop every other day to empty the little rectangular mystery hole. Listing all the weirdness that appeared would be impossible. But titles give some idea: *Dharma Combat, Hungry Maggot, Hotel Dire, Dunk and Piss, The Mad Farmers' Jubilee Almanack, Quest For Sex, Moon Rust, Croatan Express, Dreem Virus, 2-Ton Santa, Heliophobe, What in Tard Nation, Bimbox, Murder Can Be Fun, The Eulessynian Hot Tub Mystery Religion.*

My favorites included *These Exit Times* – the official organ of VHEMT (the Voluntary Human Extinction Movement, whose slogan was "Live Long and Die Out") and *Snuff It – the Journal of the Church of Euthanasia* (slogan: "Save the Planet Kill Yourself.") I also received the complete forensic photos of all Jeffrey Dahmer's victims, with a note asking if I wanted to trade. It wasn't clear what this necroperv thought I had, and that one got tossed before I left the post office. Most scabrous and hilarious was *Mondo BM*, twenty-two scratchy drawings with insane captions regarding the miraculous power of human feces.

However, by far the most important to me was the *Moorish Science Monitor*. This zine (8 ½ by 11, folded and stapled on the crease) included a communiqué proposing a Congress of Weird Religions. I recognized the writer's name. Hakim Bey was the personage who'd loved my work and wanted more for *Semiotexte(e) USA*. In his communiqué, he called for a convocation of what he called the Free Religions, namely the Psychedelic and Discordian churches, neo-pagan covens, antinomian heretics, Kaos Magicians, revolutionary Hoodooers, unchurched and anarchist Christians, practitioners of Magical Judaism, followers of the SubGenius gospel, radical Taoists, and the Moorish Orthodox Church. Just the names of these farflung Krazy Kults made my head swim with visions. I wrote back, saying I wanted in.

At the epicenter of the zine phenomenon was *Factsheet Five*, a review organ that covered hundreds of self-published works in every issue. Showing up at the *F-S 5* parties was a way to put faces with all the pseudonyms, incognitos, aliases, and implausible titles of nobility. At one of these gatherings, I discovered that Debby Schwartz-Doppelganger, Rabbi Jon-9, and Joe Bastard Armpit were all the same guy, and that he was responsible for the current incarnation of the *Moorish Science Monitor*. There, among the zine freaks, dopers and drunks, mad prophets, gay blades, and UFO contactees, I met Hakim Bey.

He emerged from a cloud of smoke in a caftan and fez: half magus and half mirage. In that moment, the power and allure of Moorish regalia was fully revealed. The fez, or tarboosh, is a brimless cone-shaped flat-crowned hat usually with a tassel. Proudly worn by Hakim Bey, it was both symbol and sorcery. No one (not even Boris Karloff in *The Mummy*) did more to make the fez the headgear of the supernally hip.

The next morning a select group retired to a local diner for the Brunch of the Gods. Over heaps of bacon and home fries, pancakes and eggs, and endless cups of coffee, Hakim Bey told me that the next time I was in New York City, I should look him up.

Letters made their way back and forth, and after a few months, I searched him out, in upper Manhattan, in the neighborhood he called Crackopolis. He had only one room then, furnished entirely with tottering stacks of books, drifts of writing paper, and layers of ash-coated Persian carpets. He had no bed, sleeping in this nest of chaos.

Next time, my host told me, I shouldn't get out of my car. There on West 107th, it would get stolen in five minutes. Better for me to beep the horn and he'd come down to greet me.

Again, he'd appeared from a cloud of smoke. Mostly, it was hand-rolled tobacco haze, but also pearly-blue cannabis fumes, incense from India, a pinch of loose sizzled gunpowder, and a pungent friable substance which I was never been able to identify.

He spoke at length. Except the warning about my car, however, much of what he said vaporized and has drifted off from memory.

This much I recall: I told him that I'd visited the Cathedral of St. John the Divine before finding my way to his place. There, I paid my respects at the cathedral's shrine for Brother John Coltrane. Other jazz musicians had mystique and maniacal followers, but there was a genuine religion devoted to Trane, the mightiest tenor sax player who ever lived. The cathedral had plenty of space, in the countless side chapels and grottos, for any type of devotion or worship that appealed to the residents of New York City's drug-infested slumscape.

The cathedral had been consecrated in 1911, a supposedly magical year. Only much later did Hakim Bey explain the significance of that date. St. John the Divine was never completed, and it never would be. The Episcopalians ran out of money and the neighborhood slowly went to hell. Still, he made the claim that though unfinished, it was the largest gothic cathedral in the world.

INITIATION

Hakim Bey's summoning flyer hung in the closet I'd converted into a tiny office. It was thumbtacked to a board, just over my right shoulder as I pounded out the rough draft of my novel *Big Gurl* on a Royal manual typewriter. As other items were added and removed, his invitation acquired pinholes and small circles of thumbtack rust, as though used for target practice by an army of commando elves.

At my request, Hakim Bey wrote a blurb for the book. The publisher, however, rejected it and slapped banal pop fiction bumf on the back cover. Dated March 15, 1988, the original blurb appears here for the first time in its entirety.

BIG GURL — never before have I come across such a vivid exposé of the Horrors of Heterosexuality — the Twilit World of Oedipal Normalcy. Young boys need it special, as Uncle Bill would say. Comrades, if you were beginning to wonder why you're queer, read on ... and regain your faith through this prose equivalent of R. Crumb and S. Clay Wilson stoned on evil speed and sterno. Eeeuuw!

About this time, he bought a ramshackle cottage in the Catskills, creating his secret ashram, the Hun-T'un Hermitage. He invited me to come and visit, and I stayed at this place – in a cluster of summer-use-only hovels far above Greenwood Lake — many times. The house was ripe with omnipresent woodsy dampness and the man-funk of unwashed anarchists. Besides burnt tobacco, cannabis and incense, there was a Franklin stove in one corner of the main room, with doors that never sealed tightly. Here, in this haze-laden den, masculine grime mingled with esoteric thought. Legends were exhumed and examined. Dirty jokes were flung into the smoky atmosphere, along with secret surmises and that most all-American of folk-forms: high and mighty bullshit.

It was at the Hun-T'un Hermitage that I first read *Temporary Autonomous Zone*, still in typescript. I'd slept on the porch in clammy sheets that had been used dozens of times and was up early, while the others slept off the night's tale-telling and revels. I lay on the dank, fusty bed and read — before publication — the text that would most define Hakim Bey.

What was a Temporary Autononous Zone? And why did this brainchild (more than any actual manifestation) so ensorcell the minds of dissolute poseurs and wannabe revolutionaries? It didn't hurt that the acronym — TAZ — was also the nickname of a ferocious cartoon character: the Tasmanian devil, who was as much a cyclone as a wild animal. Also, the word "chaos" (which Hakim Bey flung around in poetry and provocation) had a hip and slightly dangerous feel. Beyond that, the TAZ meant fleeting freedom, escape from the Man, weird sex, weirder drugs, fearsome fun, and secrecy. That is: if the all-seeing eye on the top of the pyramid wasn't watching, if the Powers and Principalities didn't even suspect what was going on, then one's pleasure was like a shaman's maneuver carried out at an impossible angle to the universe.

The Communiqués of the Association for Ontological Anarchy (one of his many one-man organizations) had already extended his intoxicating influence. These tracts treated such heady topics as Poetic Terrorism, Paganism, Wild Children, the Assassins, Pornography, and Sorcery. In other words, he wrote in a beautiful and cryptic way about the repressed and the forbidden. At that time, when zines were blossoming and shooting out potent seeds, when the world seemed a much bigger place, I had no idea what he was talking about, but I knew that his words (and the feel of the zines) made my brain feel buzzy and strange. Reading the manuscript for *TAZ* on Hakim Bey's fetid sleeping porch, I entered fully, for the first time, into his imaginal realm.

Up well before the others, I went out to the patio to breathe fresher, cooler, air. It had rained overnight and the patio was still wet. A few beer cans were scattered among the piles of last year's rotted leaves, glasses half full with brownish water, scummy puddles, broken flower pots, and dead plants. The previous owner had left a tumbledown BBQ altar with a few bricks missing. Inside were the sodden remains of a month-old bonfire.

I found some firecrackers left over from the night before, and, using a steak knife, slit them lengthwise and scraped out the gray crystals. Saltpeter, sulfur and carbon black: damp but not utterly ruined. I pushed together a little pile of the gun powder and struck a match to it. A flash and sizzle and the intoxicating aromatic sourish smoke: a smell of childhood, wild fun, and freedom. All alone in the early morning damp, I breathed deep the heady fumes.

Later that day, we went in search of some scopophiliac pleasures. That is, we took a trip to investigate the ruins of an old cement factory. With its tottering cyclopean walls and arches of rotting stone, this would have served as a perfect location for a story by H.P. Lovecraft. It was easy to imagine it as the ancient worship site for some gibbering Cthulhu cult. Before the Borscht Belt resorts, before weekenders from Manhattan came hunting for antiques, the Catskills were the abode of wild inbred hillbillies, carriers of so-called vicious protoplasm.

Lovecraft's mania about incest and racial degeneration takes its most wretched form in the these hills. Not Arkham and Innsmouth, but the hills and rocky kills broken by waterfalls, where lost clans (the Jukes, the Kallikaks, the Nams and the Jackson Whites) made their last stand. This was cacogenic country: the land of forbidden race-mixing and degenerate protoplasm.

That night at the Hun-T'un Hermitage, I was initiated into the Moorish Orthodox Church. The others enjoyed liquor and high grade cannabis. (I was totally straight-edge abstinent in those days.) Hakim Bey put on his fez and declared me a Moor. Certain phrases in dog-Arabic were intoned. Crytpic hand-jives were performed, like those of Mandrake the Magician, whose main weapon was to gesture hypnotically. And so I was officially a Moor, free to use that word however I liked.

Hakim Bey took a long drag on his pipe, and read from a tattered document. A Moor, he asserted, might belong to any religion or none. The Moorish Orthodox Church sought out the universal spirit hidden anywhere, revealed in all cultures. Occult and dissident, it was an invisible college embracing East and West but rejecting any official stultifying Consensus Reality.

Implausible or not, the proper paperwork to found the Ziggurat Lodge of the MOC was bestowed upon me by direct transmission (and bears the stamp of a genuine notary public.) Along with Hakim Bey, other Moorish Nobles (including Harpocrates "Harpo" Ben Ishmael Bey) put their signatures to my diploma.

And I was in.

BACK FROM THE SHADOWS

Besides my diploma, I brought home with me another copy of *The Moorish Science Monitor*, the issue that had begun the rebirth of the MOC. It's only two sheets, xeroxed on both sides and folded, making eight pages, without even a staple to bind the leaves. The images crammed inside include a handsome black man in a fez and robe, Taoist hell money, the cover from a hoodoo policy player's dream book, a traditional Chinese medicine chart, palm trees beneath a lovely crescent moon, and al Buraq (the magical beast which the Prophet Mohammed rode on his night journey to the heavens.) Every bit of space that's not filled with these fuzzy xeroxed pictures is packed with demands (*We want sacred madness!*) and announcements:

Editorial

In the 18 years since the last issue of the Moorish Science Monitor appeared (in Baltimore) the Moorish Orthodox Church has continued to exist – somnolent perhaps but not totally dormant. The Manhattan lodge has maintained its continuity, and all over the U.S.A. individuals still remember – once a Moor, always a Moor!

We're just as proud of our roots in the psychedelic churches movement of the '60s (Ananda Ashram,

League for Spiritual Discovery, etc.) as we are of our even deeper wellspring in the Moorish Science Temple and the teachings of Noble Drew Ali, which date back to 1913. But we've never held to any dogma or ritual, and there's no reason why the MOC should be defined by its past.

Considering that the Church's great talent has always lain in doing nothing whatsoever, but only in being, how then do we propose to adapt Moorish Orthodoxy to meet the spiritual needs of the '80s? We don't. Moorish Orthodoxy is already perfect and needs no change. All we propose to do is make it a bit more visible, and a bit more actively-inactive (as the taoists say.)

Church Announces Membership Drive

Most people don't need to know anything about Moorish Science in order to decide whether to embrace it or repudiate it. Many Moors have become instant converts simply by hearing the very words "Moorish Orthodox Church of America" – and only later (if ever) bothered to find out why.

The ancient Gnostics believed that some humans are naturally already saved – all they need is to hear the Call and at once they remember their true identities. That's the way most of us feel about the MOC.

If you are beginning to get this feeling, O new reader, brother/sister, then you may want to know how to become a Moor and start your own temple.

Moorish-American Hand of Friendship Extended to all Englighted Faiths.

Our ecumenicalism is tempered by our general lack of enthusiasm for all organized religions. Enlightened Faith by our definition means heresy or non-authoritarian new religion or crackpot cult with only one member. We may be Orthodox by name but we're heterodox by conviction. Our members are free to belong to other faiths as well – but the MOC in itself considers itself outside all religious law.

THE PROPHET

A true American paragon, Noble Drew Ali could have stepped from the pages of Melville or Ishmael Reed, a thought of Allah clothed in flesh, a fact, a poetic fact. The most famous photo of this Moorish prophet shows a dignified black man dressed in a robe, sash and fez, with his right hand placed over his solar plexus, like a mystic Napoleon from Morocco.

To recover the meaning of this obscure and enigmatic portrait, Hakim Bey claimed, we must rediscover a lost or secret portion of our own history, which is defined as much by its absences and disappearances as by its official presences. Indeed, perhaps even more so.

At age twenty-seven, in Newark, New Jersey, Noble Drew Ali had a dream in which he was ordered to found a religion for the uplifting of fallen mankind, and especially for the lost-found nation of American blacks. He obeyed the dream-command, establishing The Moorish Science Temple, which taught that blacks were not Negroes but Asiatics. To further confound their enemies and delight their friends, these new/old Moors also taught that Celts were Asiatics too. (Thus, given the Scottish ancestors on my mother's side, I could in good faith claim to be a

Moor.) According to original homeland and Moorish-American as our true nationality.

Facts and fiction, for Hakim Bey, were opposites only in the way images in a mirror oppose the so-called real world. He was convinced that one of Noble Drew Ali's craziest ideas would turn out to be sheer fact, expressed in religious metaphors, viz: evidence pointed toward a prehistoric link between Morocco and Ireland. There was truth of an esoteric nature in Noble Drew Ali's teachings about Ireland being once part of the Moorish Empire, Saint Patrick's banishing of the snakes as a mask for expulsion of the Irish Moors, and the Celts as an Asiatic race. And there was evidence that the Prophet had heard these secrets from authentic folk sources.

One of the most compelling clues was found in music. Hakim Bey heard it in the eerie similarity between Moroccan Berber music and Irish *sean-nós* or chant-style singing. He explored this on his late night show, The Moorish Orthodox Radio Crusade. Using folk tunes collected in Ireland and comparing it with Gnaoua, Joujouka, High Atlas Berber, and other Moroccan musics, he proclaimed the similarities to be unmistakable.

My first taste of Moorish music came courtesy of a Welsh rock and roller. I bought a copy of *Brian Jones Presents the Pipes of Pan at Joujouka* when I was a teenager. Not long before, I'd heard a record of Bird and Diz doing "A Night in Tunisia," a swinging slice of North African hipster bebop. But Joujouka was the real thing, even if filtered through a Rolling Stone's drug-addled imagination. Jones had gone to Morocco and taped the Master Musicians (described by William Burroughs as a 4,000 year-old rock and roll band) during their Rites of Pan (that is: goat god) festival. The music, and the rites it accompanied, reveal a glimpse of pagan North Africa barely hidden under the ragged cloak of Islam. Brian Jones' version, released on the Stones' private label three years after it was recorded, had phasing and echo and intrusive edits, which muddied the effect. Still, the sound of the call and response singing, the skirling double reeds, drones, panpipes, and trance-inducing drums came through and gave me a yen for Moroccan exotica.

A few years before, I'd had my first encounter with the word "Moor." Published in 1965, *Durango Street* is the story of a black gang which claimed that name for themselves. I was drawn to this teen novel because of the violence (quite tepid by current standards) and its glimpse of urban delinquent life. Why had tough, knife-wielding street kids call themselves the Moors? Only vague references are made to North African pirates – but clearly, bad-ass cool and darkness of skin were factors. There's even a girl gang associated with them, the Am-Moors (the Lovers.)

The word "Moor" has a tangled and tainted history, wandering in a half dozen directions. Ultimately it's derived from the Latin *Mauri*, used by the Romans to describe the inhabitants of northwest Africa, which in classical times constituted the Imperial province of Mauritania. In Spanish, *Morisco* meant Muslim. A Maroon, in the New World, was a fugitive slave or a descendent of such slaves, or someone put on a desolate place, such as a desert island, and abandoned there. (This meaning goes back to *cimmaron*: wild and unruly.) Maroon is also a dark wine red, that is, the color of the traditional Moroccan fez.

The moors of England are tracts of open rolling heathery wasteland, broken by neolithic sites and peat bogs. England is also the home of Morris dancing. This folk form, with bizarre costumes and old English tunes, goes back to an imitation of Moorish dance, or so the English of the sixteenth century conceived it. And there's also Othello, the Moor of Venice, often played in blackface, hyper-macho, and consumed with homicidal jealousy.

In short, "Moor" meant exotic, full of power, mysterious, and sometimes damned. The Moorish Science Temple was grounded on these shifting cultural sands. Myth and legend, tales and contradictions make up the history of the Temple's founder, who is thought by his followers to have been born Timothy Drew in 1886. Some claim he was the child of former slaves in a Cherokee tribe. Others were convinced he was the son of a mixed-race father and full-blooded Native American. In any case, Noble Drew Ali was the founder of the Moorish Science Temple, and by the time of his death at age 43, had tens of thousands of followers in seventeen temples throughout the midwest and upper south.

Like Hakim Bey, Drew Ali was initiated into a number of secret societies. He was a Pythian Knight, a Prophet of the Veiled Realm, a Shriner, and a thirty-second degree Mason. He declared that he'd traveled to Egypt, where he'd met a high priest of ancient magic. He was recognized by this shadowy figure as the reincarnation of Jesus, the Buddha, and Muhammed. He was also entrusted with a so-called lost section of the *Quran*, which came to be known as the *Holy Koran of the Moorish Temple of America*. I first heard of this text by the name "Circle Seven Koran" (called this because of its cover, which shows a red number 7 surrounded by a blue circle.)

My copy was passed on to me by Hakim Bey. A tattered xerox made in the '70s, it's hard to decipher. The toner dissolves into dust as I turn the pages and the paper has taken on a yellowy parchment hue. At first glance, it might be a book lost for hundreds of years, exhumed from a secret tomb.

Moorish Orthodoxy was founded originally to explore the esoteric dimensions of Noble Drew's teachings, discovered in such passages from the "Circle Seven Koran" as these:

> *Now cease to seek for heaven in the sky;*
> *Just open up the windows of your heart and*
> *like a flood of light, a heaven will come and*
> *bring a boundless joy.*

Regarding doctrine of the lost/found church, Hakim Bey proclaimed that there was absolutely none. Moorish Orthodoxy is like a mirror in which each seeker beholds a beloved form, each one different. There is no required ritual and no source of authority other than those the individual imagination provides.

To help restore their true identity, early members of the Temple were given new names and ID cards, so-called passports. Mine has three symbols emblazoned on the top — a crescent moon with a star at one point, a pair of clasped hands, and the number seven with a scaly circle around it like the snake that eats its own tail. The word "Unity" is printed over the shaking hands, and below that is my Moorish name.

Below this is the following declaration:

This is your nationality and identification card for the Moorish Science Temple of America, and birthright for the Moorish Americans. We honor the divine prophets Jesus, Mohammed, Buddha and Confucius. May the blessings of the God of our Father ALLAH be upon you that carry this card. I do hereby declare that you are a Muslim under the Divine Law of the Holy Koran of Mecca — Love, Truth, Peace, Freedom and Justice. "I am a citizen of the U.S.A." Noble Drew Ali, the Prophet.

Though the prophet's 1929 death certificate states that he succumbed to tuberculosis broncho-pneumonia after being in police custody, a simpler and more plausible explanation is traditional American Death By Cop.

MOORISH MAIL-ORDER MYSTICISM

The clandestine network of zines brought me into contact with living MOC members. And zines continued to prod and poke at my mind. When I asked Hakim Bey about this, he had a long and convoluted answer.

Moorish Mail-order Mysticism might have sounded like a joke, but the Moorish Orthodox Church took it seriously. There was something magical about the mail. You have to be dead to make it onto a U.S. stamp – dead or mythic. Voices from the unseen – documents as amulets – and something very American, democratic and self-reliant. Mysterious urban folklore – old ads in crumbling yellow magazines – Hoodoo catalogues and dream books.

I'd driven down for another weekend of palaver and esoteric exploration. At times, it felt as though his utterances came like the Pope's — *ex cathedra* — though stretched out recumbent in his book-strewn upper chamber, this might be more accurately called *ex lectus* (from the bed.) I scribbled some notes, trying to catch his wandering lines of thought. I listened far more than I spoke. His vocabulary and phrasing, his cadences of speech, were becoming my own: apostolic succession through the spoken word.

Ancient spirits-of-place intersecting with modern communication networks that are placeless – spooky and abstract. And now the mail itself seems antique – a lost modernity – 19th century, sepia, violet ink – a fitting medium for the transmission of secrets.

As he spoke, I murmured back an echo – call and response, like a Baptist preacher lining out a hymn for illiterate believers.

Why not do-it-yourself enlightenment? It may not be the best way or the only way, but it is a way. A genuine vein of initiation runs from the plane where we find Dr. Bronner's soap labels — the lost Books of Moses — Hollow Earth Theory — mail-order courses of Druids and occult orders — millenarian tracts – sexy Mexican lithographs. A field of magical correspondences.

Hakim Bey took a pleasurable draw and exhaled a thin string of smoke, reminding me of the nineteenth century drawings of Santa Claus with his long-stemmed pipe and scraggly beard.

The mail is full of gnostic traces – even of love. Why not initiation? It all adds up to the New World Religion – a playground for the Trickster. Literal belief in one or another of these mail-order revelations would destroy the ability to believe in all of them simultaneously. However we could embrace BOTH/AND rather than EITHER/OR.

Again came the meandering trail of images which I struggled to absorb.

Egyptomania – the imaginal Islam of old cigarette boxes and Masonic bric-a-brac – the Hoodoo figure of the Old Moor – Jewish magic and amulets – mail-order almanacs of chaos cults from the Seven Finger High Glister of the Great Dismal Swamp.

He leaned back and gave a wry smile, imitating a snake oil salesman winding up his spiel. *And all this can now be yours, as you Send Away For a Split-Second of Eternity!*

Amusing nonsense or secret wisdom? Or perhaps something that could include nuggets of glittering bullshit *and* swollen veins of revelation?

A rare silence filled the space between us. Then I made bold to ask about the earliest days of the Moorish Orthodox Church. He settled back on his bed to tell the tale of Warren Tartaglia, or Walid al-Taha, as he was known to the Moorish brethren.

He lived up in the Bronx. He was from a lower middle class background — Italian. He was extremely brilliant, one of the most brilliant people I ever knew. He read everything that we hadn't, constantly telling us what we should read. Things like Hermann Broch and Malaparte, al-Gahzali. He was also a jazz musician, playing beautiful soprano sax — good enough to play with Art Blakey.

And he was a junkie, eventually dying of an overdose at age twenty-one. But he was the one who set the fashion that we all followed. We all talked like him, using his expressions.

He knew Rafi Sharif (Rafi was from Baltimore). How they met I don't know. Rafi was a little older than us. He went to military academy and then somehow he got fascinated by the Moorish Science Temple. Rafi had gotten himself accepted by the temple elders in Baltimore and inducted into the religion. He was Jewish but he converted to Islam. I forget what his birth name was but it might've been Yale Singer. He called himself Yael Sharif at one point.

Rafi had founded several offshoots of the Moorish Science Temple for hipsters — this was '62, '63, '64 — including the Noble Order of Sufis and the Moorish Orthodox Church, along with Greg Foster, who was a junkie poet we knew. They had combined the wandering bishop Orthodox Christianity with Moorish Science.

Science? Not test tubes, Frankenstein's life-giving lightning, nor particle physics. Science in this case meant knowledge, something to be studied and treasured. Moorish understanding – Moorish wisdom. Every time we met or spoke on the phone, every time he replied to my letters or I replied to his, sparks of gnosis jumped the gap, a flicker of illumination or ignition.

The Church more or less abandoned all orthodoxy (though not the name) and found its true spirit in Sufism, of various unorthodox varieties, including Isma'ílism (the teachings of the Assassins). But many other strains were woven into the MOC in the '60s, including Advaita Vedanta, Tantra, Neo-American-style psychedelic mysticism, Native American symbolism, and insurrectionary activism.

CHAOS

So, is this all just cultural appropriation? Elvis got smeared with this crusty brush, condemned for ripping off black musicians and giving them no credit for their influences. Countless white rock bands too have been outed as mere poseurs who built their entire careers on the work of penniless bluesmen.

There is of course much truth in such recrimination, especially when trillions of dollars are at stake. Yet America is built on theft. Armed robbery is the defining principle of this country. Europeans did, after all, appropriate the land of the indigenous peoples. And Europeans did of course appropriate the lives of millions of African slaves. Without these atrocities America would just be a place where English cod fishers stopped to fill their water casks.

It's the way it works here. America is a vast, snarled knot of thievery, adoption, imitation, plagiarizing, loan, debt, plunder, poaching, cultural kleptomania. Call it whatever you want. But to claim primacy or ownership is a tiresome waste of time.

Of course jazz is black, America's greatest contribution to world culture. Yet without European brass instruments left over from the Great Slave Holder's Rebellion (sometimes known as the Civil War) — no such thing. And without the great Jewish tunesmiths (e.g: George Gershwin, nee Jacob Gershowitz, and Irving Berlin, nee Israel Beilin) the harmonies of jazz might never have progressed beyond the blues.

Santa Claus and the Christmas tree: thank the Germans. The rites and costumes of the Catholic church – most of this comes from ancient Rome. Puerto Ricans wearing green plastic hats on St. Patrick's Day. Scottish bagpipes playing at a Polish fireman's funeral. Kung-fu and karate, chihuahuas and Great Danes, chess and the tarot, mayonnaise and hamburgers, white suburban college kids celebrating the Mexican Day of the Dead with tributes to David Bowie, catsup, sherbet, algebra, saunas, yoga, and yogurt: the list is endless.

Hakim Bey asked if I knew that Saint Patrick was also Damballa in Trinidadian hoodoo. This was in a letter, but still I could see him smiling three hundred miles away.

Everything was – or could be – connected and layered together. Everything, that is, which interested him in the moment. Santa Claus was identified as the spirit of fly agaric – a hallucinogenic mushroom. (They're both red with white highlights, and very trippy.) Mercury was not only Thoth and Hermes but also the Hindu god/planet Budh, actively worshipped in India today. Budh was the bastard love-child of Soma the moon and Tara the star.

So, in that long tradition of stealing with both hands, how much of Hakim Bey's considerable literary output is just cultural theft and flimflam? How much of my Moorish identity is simply All-American bunkum? Appropriation can be a tangled web — equal parts delight and guilt, but Hakim Bey wanted nothing to do with gazing stupidly at other cultures or trying to tap their spiritual sap without paying any karmic dues.

While some might call this mere wishful thinking, others see Hakim Bey as a master of syncretism: the integration of different (often seemingly irreconcilable) religious ideas and practices.

Catholic saint lore + west African religion = voodoo.

Freemasonry + America folk magic + the King James Bible = Mormonism.

The square root of hillbilly spunk x cranked-up rhythm and blues = rock and roll

These formulae may not be common knowledge, but they aren't esoteric secrets either. Hakim Bey took syncretism farther than most, blending mythic, historical, and psycho-geographical flights of fancy. With a straight face, he insisted that the Munsee-Mohican Bear God was actually Bacchus — who was also Shiva, the Celtic Cernunnos, and Herne the Hunter — the Paleolithic animal-master god, consort of the Willendorf Venus. Proof? He claimed to have two Indian informants.

This mode of thinking is further developed in a document (printed on lavender paper) called "Episcopaganism: for the Repaganization of Monotheism." Moorish Orthodox Church = Theosophico-Masonic Aquarian Gospel + Black Islam + Cherokee shamanism + Wandering Bishop apostolic succession + heterodox sufism + psychedelic sacrament.

When he was a boy of ten or eleven his family went on vacation to New Orleans, and there he had discovered Voodoo, and insisted on being taken to the grave of Marie Laveau. Looking back on this later he realized that this occult pilgrimage had constituted (after singing in an Episcopalian boys' choir) his second occult initiation, and his first affiliation with Afro-American tradition.

The mailman brought me another over-ripe example of his cross-cultural mishmashing, a letter with one-of-a-kind *Celtic Alginkin Hoodoo & Neo-Pagan Anabaptist Convention* letterhead, replete with hand-drawn stars.

There was for him some tiptoeing and muted discomfort concerning the question of cultural appropriation. Yet he never hung back from enjoying what others had to offer. Chinese eels in inky sauce, Sun Ra's Afro-Cosmic jazz, Amish community (especially the bee, where work is done with much conviviality and fatty food), lounging about in a Javanese sarong, trailer trash boys wearing proud mullets, southern fried chicken, Santeria and hoodoo and German pietist mysticism. He had no real claim to any of these. But who does anymore? And more importantly — who cares?

Let 1000 flowers (or weeds) bloom! – so he proclaimed. That included syncretisms, mixtures and impurities. Difference and solidarity versus sameness and separation: that was his position in a nutshell. Sufism, Irish folk tales, witchlore, alchemical formulations, cave paintings, and Mennonite hymnody: these all found a place in his self-created mythos.

At the time I was granted my Ziggurat Lodge MOC charter, I still clung to notions of cultural purity. That is, I thought there were such things as art, music, and foodways untainted by corrupting outside influences. I knew the twisted histories of jazz and pizza, Christmas trees, Saint Patrick's Day, Chef Boyardee spaghetti, and Tex-Mex polka. Yet I hung onto the idea that certain types of American folk music had some sort of purity. I sneered at my bandmates about white guys playing what I called fake reggae and bogus funk.

But all my rigid puritanical claims missed the point. Was Bix Beiderbecke (the greatest jazz cornetist, ever) stealing from black culture (and Claude Debussy)? Yes – no – and what difference does it make? Does any culture have sole ownership of coffee? Should black people not enjoy Santa Claus or Elvis? Yoga and yogurt – these are world-wide phenomena, not the property of certain Asian ethnic groups.

It took me years to see the charm, the power, the beauty, in scrambled culture and the chaotic mishmash of traditions. Hakim Bey's book, *Chaos,* which loomed out of the shadows in 1985, was crucial to this change. Published by the Grim Reaper Press in

Providence, it's only 28 pages long. But line for line, phrase for phrase, no book has had a stronger influence on me as a writer. Sometimes classified as a collection of rants, *Chaos* is far more than that: with a hundred times the gorgeous weirdness of countless so-called Great Books. Most of these short poetic screeds made their presence known first in zines, floating like spectral spoors in the U.S. postal system. The language is exquisite; the subject matter is strange and at times disturbing. I read this book again and again.

My facsimile edition (with a hot pink cover) contains the following publication statement: *No copyright 1985. May be freely pirated and quoted – however the author and publisher would like to be informed at* (Here follows a blank space.) *Also, no ISBN number, no Library of Congress catalog number, no Imprimatur, no Nihil Obstat. Manufactured in Hyperborea.*

Later, Hakim Bey gave me a recording of himself, intoning his spell of invocation. *Chaos never died. Primordial uncarved block, sole worshipful monster, inert and spontaneous, more ultraviolet than any mythology (like the shadows before Babylon) the original and undifferentiated oneness-of-being still radiates serene as the black pennants of the Assassins, random and perpetually intoxicated. Chaos comes before all principles of order and entropy.*

Ruminating aloud, he asked whether we needed a defense of filth, as fertility, as pleasure, as relaxation from the rigidities of civilization. Not nostalgia for the mud, but the mud itself.

Another of his phrases — *the placental wetness of becoming* — was both distressing and an inspiration. When he asserted that juice and slime are the ultimate free-form connective and penetrative tissues of living systems, it seemed a rather elaborate way of praising messes and messing around. Still, the words stayed with me, and the meaning slowly seeped into the hidden places in my brain.

POETIC FACTS

Religion is magic theater, just as theater was originally magical religion. Ritual is the chief and perhaps sole raison d'etre for religion because ritual is, or at least sometimes can be, magic.

Making the word "magick," Aleister Crowley added the letter K to differentiate it from mere stage flummery. But with that one letter he created something far more baffling than pulling rabbits out of hats or sawing ladies in half. Crowley was a sorcerer, in a way not dissimilar to Noble Drew Ali, Mandrake the Magician, Houdini, the Mormon Prophet Joseph Smith, and Hakim Bey.

When a religion from one culture penetrates another culture, it frequently does so (at least initially) as heresy. Only later do the religious goon squads arrive to straighten everyone out and make them toe the line. A good example is early Celtic Christianity, which absorbed a great deal of Druidry, and was seen from Rome as heretical.

Hakim Bey's studies of heresy took him deep into apocrypha, pornographic comic books, heraldic symbolism, throw-away arcana, and occult pamphleteering. Excluded and excoriated by academics, he was far more interested in discovering poetic facts, weaving a spell out of scholarly dust and old cobwebs, than in standard bloodless historical work. In America, the concept of the independent scholar is a null set, and he had to use his imagination more than so-called real historians would allow, erecting a lot of suppositions on a shaky framework and adding a glistening dollop of fantasy. Reveries, childhood dreams, fancies and magical images – these can provide us with deeper truth than the dreary grindhouse of academic research.

It wasn't the pure that he was interested in. It was the real, a new synthesis rather than simply a mishmash of styles, a pattern of conversions, of literal crosscultural adventures. And Noble Drew Ali was a real American prophet, the black man with a Cherokee feather stuck in his fez. He was the perfect image of everything Hakim Bey wished America were and sadly isn't.

He carefully handed me a flimsy sheet of paper and told me again that the shamanic trace is in all religions.

How this tattered flyer got into his hands, I can not explain. But clearly it had been passed as a precious relic from Moor to Moor for almost a hundred years. At the top is the bold heading in German black letter: "Don't Miss the Great Moorish Drama. Look! Look! Come ye everyone and see The Seventh Wonder of the World. The great Moorish drama which constitutes Events in the Last Days Among the Inhabitant of North America." Taking up a third of the page is a picture of Noble Drew Ali in fez, robe and sash.

The text I reproduce here verbatim:

In this Moorish drama, the need of a nationality will be made known to you through the acts of men, women and children. There will be great lectures and this great Nationalistic topic by the Prophet Noble Drew Ali, and many of the Sheiks of the Grand Body of the Moorish Holy Temple of Science. You will also hear one of the greatest Moorish female songstresses of our day — Mme. Lomax Bey. The Prophet Noble Drew Ali will be bound with several yards of rope, as Jesus was bound at the temple in Jerusalem. And escaped before the Authorities could take charge of Him. So will the Prophet Noble Drew Ali perform the same act, after being bound by anyone in the audience and will escape in a few seconds. He will also heal many in the audience without touching them free of charge, as they stand in front of their seats manifesting his divine power. Come One, Come All to the Moorish Holy Temple of Science at Community Center 3140 Indiana Avenue. 8 to 10 pm. Refreshments served. Admission: Adults 50c Children 25c. On Monday evening. May 16th, 1927.

Shamanism appears as trickery to modern Western observers, often making use of sleight of hand as a therapeutic and thaumaturgic tactic. It's not superstition nor fraud, but rather a deeply-rooted secret in all healing faiths. So it was that two years before his death, with dozens of temples established in cities throughout the U.S., the prophet was still doing what might be called stage magic.

TRUE DESIRES

Some have called Hakim Bey a chameleon: reflecting back the fascinations of those around him at any given moment. He was called a saint and a fraud, a genius and a plagiarist – and this by one of his dearest friends.

On occasion I did see him slide effortlessly from one persona to another. When young acolytes showed up at his door, eager for illumination, he could put on the robes of the Great Hipster Wizard, spieling away about anarchism, situationism, immediatism, and other fleeting hip-isms. When chowing down in a diner with friends of his generation, he'd spin out tales of '60s-era self-indulgence, replete with dope lore and obscure name-droppings. Worst was when critical theory raised its hideous head, toothless and bleary-eyed. I had enough perspective to see how the hippest jargon goes stale the quickest. Stuck listening to self-important ideologues driveling on about Baudrillard and Foucault, I ventured to say that no one was more provincial than a Parisian intellectual. This didn't even get me a blank or contemptuous stare from the critical theory mavens. It seemed to me all a fuzzy footnote to Nietzsche. Hakim Bey heard me, and shrugged off my comment. Like a jellyfish, he could bob and sway, swish and float, in the lukewarm water of faddish ideology.

I don't claim absolute knowledge or complete understanding. But I did spend most of my time with him one on one (trying to avoid social gatherings with wearisome strangers) and there was little need for putting on airs with me. Books I should read? Yes, please, tell me more. Tales of Moorish weirdness? I was always eager for those. Almost-lost history, local sites of occult interest, forbidden lore? That's why I drove six hours downstate and was willing to sleep in his dank, bug-infested lower chambers.

Theory was not mere show for him. At least in the moment, it mattered to him. His aesthetic pronouncements and political critique were genuine, and at times astute and bitterly hilarious. But far more significant was something much simpler and much deeper.

He wanted pleasure – now, and in the real world, not in some attenuated vaporous heaven. He wanted pleasure — literal, physical, and immediate (that is, unmediated by technology.) He had little sympathy for the Buddhist critique of craving. In fact, true desire was not the enemy, but at the heart of what it meant to be human.

Watching him devour a half of a roasted duck – in a Chinatown hole-in-the-wall – was a revelation. With fat-smeared fingers, glistening lips, goo-spattered beard, he was suffused with genuine joy. On a summer night, strolling back to his place on the

Wallkill, we stopped for milkshakes. He yanked off the plastic lid, tossed away the miserly straw – which only served to regulate his pleasure – and guzzled it straight and sloppy. He told me once that when he could use the computer to get fried chicken, I should let him know. He didn't mean delivery by a sullen slacker but hot, greasy southern fried chicken coming straight out of the screen and into his hands.

This could be dismissed as mere gluttony. But I used the word "revelation" and I stand by it. When Hakim Bey called for amazement, excess, superabundance, it wasn't hype or poetic hyperbole. When he demanded marvelous secrets this wasn't just a request to try some exotic dish from an obscure cuisine. Food was one way to ecstasy, but there were others: yearning, unconquerable desire, mad love. He scoffed at the dead hand of social norms, and sometimes even at the laws of physics. The impossible? He brushed away such doubts. What else could we hope to attain but the impossible? Should we wait for someone else to reveal our true desires?

SEVENTEEN MESSENGERS

The longest we ever went on talking was thirteen hours straight. He rose at noon, enjoyed a cigarette, a few hits off his pipe, coffee with sugar, and gave an expansive sigh, grateful again for the Four Drug Groups. We talked until one in the morning, back and forth: kitchen table to nest of Persian rugs, back to the table. His tales were tall and well told, and while sometimes implausible, they were always pleasurable. He praised certain of his favorite texts as fortuitous mistranslations. This might also describe his own exploits and self-created identity.

I thought of my visits as successive initiations, into another and yet another secret society. The combination of boyish clubhouse delight and deep esoteric research was intoxicating. I didn't join Hakim Bey in his rites of cannabis, and drank no alcohol on my visits. And though we talked at length about hallucinogens, I didn't follow him on that shimmering path. My initiations were fleeting and ancient, absurd and profound.

Like a kid wanting to hear the same bedtime story, or like a holy man who recites the same passage of scripture night after night, searching for the secret message, I asked again for the origin story of the Moorish Orthodox Church.

This time, no new facts were revealed. I heard about black Muslims, beat poets, acidheads, junkies and bikers – the same cast of characters. The MOC convened in a basement on 103rd off of Broadway. They rented a storefront and dubbed it *The Moorish Science Reading Room*. There, and in the adjoining head shop, The Crypt, the new/old Moors burned incense, smoked cannabis, gazed dreamily on the posters they'd taped to the walls, and spun out their tales of political and mystical grooviness.

However, hearing the story again, when I was told that Walid al-Taha (aka Warren Tartaglia) played soprano sax, my inner ear picked up an odd dissonance. Nothing I've read about him confirms this. All the references say he was an alto sax man. A minor discrepancy? A trivial mistake?

The soprano sax is straight, and held like a clarinet. The alto has the characteristic saxophone curves and hangs from a strap around the player's neck. Warren Tartaglia died in 1965, and by then the soprano sax revival was well underway, John Coltrane giving hipness to the formerly old-fashioned instrument. It's also entirely possible that Hakim Bey's memory (or musical vocabulary) was at fault. He mentioned that Tartaglia played with Art Blakey. This is completely plausible, as Blakey's band, The Jazz Messengers, had a revolving door policy for young players. Blakey was a great drummer, and he had a great sense for finding new talent. Dozens, perhaps a hundred or so, young jazz musicians –

black and white — had their first big break with Art Blakey. The list of guys (and it was an all-boys club) who started out with Blakey contains such greats as Wayne Shorter and Keith Jarrett, and players such as Chuck Mangione who veered off into popular success. Where is Warren Tartaglia in the Jazz Messengers roll call? Obscure, and as far as I can tell, never recorded.

The original group — called The Seventeen Messengers — was also never captured on record. Formed in 1947, this big band consisted of black guys who'd become Muslims. Like so many large groups in the waning years of swing, the Seventeen Messengers couldn't survive financially. Too many musicians to pay, and too few places to play. So, like thunder clouds that form, discharge their energy, then disappear, this legendary band had a sporadic existence. By 1950, probably before, the Seventeen Messengers dissolved into the mist, and many of the members disappeared.

However, on December 27, 1947, eight members of the band did gather in the studio. The Muslim musicians included Sahib Shihab (alto sax), Musa Kaleem (tenor sax), Abdul Hamid (trumpet), Haleen Rasheed (trombone), Ibrahim ibn Ismail (piano) and Talib Dawud (trumpet). Their leader, Art Blakey had gone to Africa and taken a new name too: Abdullah ibn Buhaina.

They recorded four tunes, which were released as 78s on the Blue Note label: "The Thin Man," "Bop

Alley," "Groove Street," and "Musa's Vision." Given that Musa is the Arabic spelling of Moses, this last cut is of particular interest. Moses on Mount Sinai meeting Jahweh in a writhing thunder cloud, or Musa Kaleem blowing hot in a smoky basement jazz club? Either/or? No – both/and.

THE ASTRAL CONVENTION

The Moorish Science Monitor came and went like a perfumed specter: a few issues gliding through the mail, then a change of winds, or planetary influences, and it disappeared. An exhaustive bibliography of the *Monitor* may never be possible, as various outposts issued their version (some only once) and then returned to the shadows.

In a long typewritten letter dated Chaos Day 1990, Hakim Bey outlined the history of the *Monitor. Founded 1965 in Baltimore, ran sporadically till 1967. Chronicled the M.O.C. lodges in Baltimore, Manhattan and Millbrook NY. About half was dada cut-ups. Revived in 1986 with a special issue for the Centennial of Noble Drew Ali, which drew in many new converts. Lodges were founded in Providence RI, Tusuque NM (the Royal Moorish Airforce under Nathaniel Tarn, poet and anthropologist), Brooklyn (Autonomedia), Bombay (under the Ismaili pir Jamal "Perfect Boy"), Chicago (the Ben Ishmael Lodge under J. Koehnline), Peoria Illinois (First Church of Moorish Science, under SF-master Philip Jose Farmer) etc. The Providence lodge under Jake Rabinowitz then took over publication and ran the MSM until 1989.*

I have in my possession an incomplete, but richly-representative archive. Two Vietnam-era copies of the original mimeographed Volume One run are printed on 8 ½ by 11 yellow paper. Both feature the *Monitor*'s slogan — *Be the First On Your Horizon to be Greeted* – and a weather report (issue #3: *the heavenly father had plenty of honey but the son has a hot disease.* Issue #4: *if it doesn't move, fondle it.*)

#3 is only two pages long, with a report on the Dalai Lama's TV interview, poems by Greg Foster, a recipe for curry ("Soul food, or, a bright light in the kitchen") an astrology update, and an advice column called Ask Dr. Zill. #3 contains actual news, of the N.Y.C. Temple being destroyed by fire and firemen. Also included are poems by Ustad Selim, more astrology (with hand-drawn illos), advice for men of draft age, and a letter to Dr. Zill which I reprint here in its entirety.

Dear Dr. Zill:

I've tried every cure, electroshock therapy, breathing in Arizona, rebaptism, without success, when I read your name scrawled on a subway toilet and decided to write. I am really 14 years old in the 8th grade and I don't have any boyfriends because I am fat and have pimples. But every morning when I awake, in the mirror I see a 70 year old man and then I am driven to the government building and told that I'm the director of the FBI. Help me.

Most Sincerely,

J. Edgar Hoover

A long period of silence ensued, as the MOC entered a state of occultation. In the shadows, Moorish forces continued to maneuver and mutate. Two decades later, after Hakim Bey had returned from the east, he struck the sparks that lit countless hand-rolled cigarettes, bowls of fine cannabis, ritual campfires, lamps and lanterns under which a new generation of Moors emerged. Many people converted to Moorish Orthodoxy simply on hearing its name or seeing a photograph of Noble Drew Ali.

The efflorescense was multi-colored and fragrant, and Hakim Bey passed along word that the MOC was rumored to be in communion with the following groups: KAOS, and the Order of Ganymede (both in the UK), the Yellow Turban Society, Discordian Zen, The Sacred Jihad of Our Lady of Perpetual Chaos, the Discordian Illuminati, the Si Fan Society of Providence, the School of Magical Judaism, the Egyptian Orthodox Church of New Zealand, the Anarcho-Taoists of Willimantic CT.

The next issue of *The Mooirsh Science Monitor* presented the least known and most precious wine, and listed the following perpetrators:

Editor in Chief, Press-lord in exile — Hakim Bey

Inky Adjutant and power-crazed tin god – Ali Hossein Abu'l Jihad

Production crew: Jacob Rabinowitz, Debbie Schwartz-Doppleganger, Pinchas Weisskopf and Walid Walid Unwaller of the Unwalled City.

A short Page One editorial by Rabbi Jon-9 sets the tone for what follows:

The invasion of light is continuous. Our organization is so vast and subtle that many of our agents are not aware of themselves as such until the moment they are needed. Every accident patterns to produce a leadership "trained" from birth.

We have no records, no recognizable hierarchy. Authentic reports by warriors and spies are openly viewed in cinemas, published as sci-fi, overheard in restaurants and played on the radio.

Works of art provide us with the clues needful to take the next step. There are no secret codes. Everything is in plain sight.

We are known by many names, some of them flattering. Among them is Moorish Orthodox Church. Selah.

What follows in this *L'Amour Moor* issue is a delightful mess. An excerpt from a scandal rag called the *Weekly World News* describes paramilitary training in Heaven, readying an army of super-angels to destroy the devil. An editorial called "Sex and the Taste of Oblivion" shares a page with reviews of other zines. Metaphysics, fringe politics, a picture of a sea creature waving a severed human head, translations from Saint John of the Cross's *Dark Night of the Soul*, from Rumi, from the Song of Solomon, and Moorish News from around the world: this issue had much to crack open my mind.

On the back page is an invitation to attend the Astral Convention. In tiny print, readers are called to join others in Antarctica. *Attention all Mutants,*

Isolated Independent Thinkers, Type 3's, SubG's, Chaos Magicians, and dreamy runaway kids – at last a party that we can ALL attend — because it's being held on the ASTRAL PLANE. Yes, your body stays comfortably home meditating or even asleep — while your AETHERIC DOUBLE zooms forth to boogie at the dreamtime ball.

Of course the astral body is impervious to temperature – and with a bit of practise you can assume any imaginable form, from a simulacrum of your physical body to a ray of orgasmic light. Come prepared to entertain as well as be entertained. Make a speech, dance, performance – bring astral intoxicants, musical instruments, pet sex-demons – Astonish us!

A page of collaged artwork shows Nan Chi Hsien Weng, aka The Taoist Santa Claus. This Old Immortal of the South Pole is said to bestow long life and happiness. His boys carry the Peaches of Eternal Life and the ling-chih fungus (the mushroom of immortality.) He is declared to be the patron saint of the Antarctic Convention and will protect all astral voyagers who invoke his aid.

This astral gathering was another of Hakim Bey's acts of willful imagination, dreamed up to fight against his isolation. Though surrounded by friends and fans, he was alone in the world. Though there were other mutants, independent thinkers, and chaos magicians he might spend time with (face to face, not just in the imaginal realms) still he did on occasion use the word "loneliness" to describe certain aspects of his earthly existence. Hence all the arcane social aggregations he concocted, and all the actual fraternal organizations he took delight in: Masons and Anti-Masons, Oddfellows, Elks, Woodsmen, Theosophists, Knights of Labor, Daughters of Isis, Black Shriners, Indian Scouts, Boy Scouts, and the Patrons of Husbandry, aka The Grange (a Masonic offshoot for farmers, based on the Eleusinian Mysteries of Demeter and passed on in Naples by a Duke to an upstate farmer.)

THE PROPHET SEZ WEAR YOUR FEZ TO THE TAZ

A sheik transported by imaginal magic to the Catskills, lolling on carpets and rolling joints and endless palaver, he was the esotericized Caliph of Spliff, slurping noodles and reminiscing about his days schmoozing in Iran with Sufi nobles and with the Shah's wife.

At a voodoo wedding ceremony in suburban New Jersey he appeared in full regalia, a handsome fez topping his formal attire. No one there cut a finer figure. At a public lecture and celebration in Cairo (the one in the Hudson Valley, not on the Nile) he explained to the gathered masses why the fez should be worn and what it truly meant. At the ordination of a renegade wandering bishop in New York City, he approached the altar in a cape and snazzy spangled fez to give his blessing.

In his *Black Fez Manifesto*, Hakim Bey takes the flat-topped felt cone as a symbol for his umpteenth D.I.Y. secret initiation society, the Anarcho-Ottoman United Front. With no members other than himself, this secret imaginal organization poses little threat to the ghostworld of fashionable ideas and images that passes nowadays for Empire. Bombs will explode, but only in his imagination. The book's cover shows a black tarboosh wrapt in gorgeous flames. The fires of revolution will erupt, though likely not spread beyond the pages of this slim volume of poetry.

On speaking tours and recordings of him reading his work, in translations into two dozen languages, misquoted in *Time Magazine*'s Cyber-Punk issue (five years after Cyber-Punk was over), through actual sales of actual books: he had a distinct presence. This all indicates his status above the cultural radar. Yet Hakim Bey did not really exist in the standard sense of the word, unless a real person can be conjured entirely out of words.

For years, he hosted a radio show on WBAI: the Moorish Orthodox Radio Crusade. I was a guest on the show once, though the substance of our conversation is long gone. Probably we talked about my third novel, *Drowning in Fire*, which features tri-racial isolates in the south Jersey swamps and an old man named Kush, who I based on Hakim Bey, and who of course wears a fez. All I recall for sure of the show are the first few moments. He lay a disc on the turntable, set the needle in the groove, and out across the greater New York City area went a strange Moorish keening. When the cut ended, my host announced that we'd been listening to his theme music, played by (there came a long pause, while he puzzled over the album sleeve, which was printed all in Arabic) *Some Old Guy in a Fez*.

The mystic headgear now crowning my skull was never worn by a real North African. It was made by the Lou-Walt Company in New York City. Inside the fez is a barely-legible label:

Organizations We Serve: fraternal, secret and religious, military, educational and civic, recreational, publicity and business.

Supplies We Manufacture: uniforms, regalia and costumes, fezzes, flags and banners, jewels, badges and buttons, emblems, insignia and implements, paraphernalia for organizational activities.

My collection of fezzes — thirteen of them — is arrayed in the uppermost room in my house. Some of them were made for Shriners (the Ismaillia, Syria, and Damascus lodges are represented). Some of them — all black — had once belonged to The Mystic Order of the Veiled Prophets of the Enchanted Realm. I have found three of these Grotto Prophet tarbooshes here in Rochester. They show up in garage sales, cheap.

The Grotto Prophets claim a link back to al-Muquanna (or Mokanna, as they call him), a heretical leader who claimed to be an incarnation of God. Condemned by orthodox Muslims, he drank poison in the year 783 rather than be executed. He was reputed to wear a covering over his face (hence the name, which means the Veiled One), either because he was so beautiful that he didn't want others to be distracted by his gorgeous visage, or because he was so ugly. Over a thousand years later, in Hamilton,

New York (an hour and half east of here), a group of Master Masons formed an exclusive club devoted to japes, pranks, and practical jokes. Wanting a more arcane and glamorous air than the original Fairchild Deviltry Society, they soon changed their name, put on the black fez and brought al-Muquanna back from his long vatic sleep.

I bought my first fez in a junk sale in a retrofitted country church in Clarendon, New York. This had been for a hundred years a place of Protestant worship, ringing with a thousand stale hymns. Now the whole church was laid out in garage-sale fashion: overloaded tables, piles of depressing detritus, boxes and bins and heaps. In the chaos of this sad useless crap I found a fez that had been worn, many years before, by a member of the Ismaillia lodge. Money changed hands and off I went.

Accompanied by Anton, my Geography Jaunt partner, I spent the whole day driving around obscure sites and occult locations, wearing the fez. With the mystic headgear in place, a stream of memory began to flow upward into consciousness.

My first glimpse of the fez had come in a little-known throwaway comedy that no one else seems to remember. Sexual exhibitionism, an absurdly convoluted caper, Victor Mature's huge gleaming teeth, and a mystery man in a mystery hat: *After the Fox* poured all of this into my still-developing twelve year old brain. The film came out in 1966. It was vouchsafed to me via TV a few years later. Though I spent endless childhood hours hunkered down before the flickering screen, almost none of it remains in my memory. But much of this movie has stuck with me for half a century.

Seeing it on TV, my young impressionable mind was swamped by images of absurdity and high octane exoticism. It's a crazed Italo-American comedy rip-off of the Pink Panther movies, staring Peter Sellers as the histrionic master criminal Aldo Venucci.

As a lure for his great desert gold robbery, Aldo positions his bait, a gorgeous dark-skinned Italiana exposing herself in the desert. At first, she's covered head to toe in a black Arab robe, though one shot shows her eyes: very knowing, cunning and confident. Suddenly, as a truck full of gold drives by, she drops the burka and shows off the amazing lush body: wide hips and full breasts (imagine Sophia Loren without the talent, charisma or a future in film.)

She's wearing an amalgam of belly dance costume, strippers' get-up, and futuristic bikini. Besides spangles, garters, dark veil, black stockings, there are vaguely chainlike elements to her costume, evoking her slave status and her enslaving nature. Hands on hips, she sways her body at the men: a taunt and a triumph of the female flesh. The gold-heisters, stupefied by the sheer power of her body, drive the truck off the road and into the trap.

The actress, Maria Grazia Buccella, had little success to speak of after this film. Here is her one moment of greatness: a flash of lush coppery curves in the desert, then throwing the robe back on.

She's the sexual property of the archetypal well-seasoned master criminal. In this case it's Akim Tamiroff, making his homage to Sidney Greenstreet: a fat, pseudo-Asiatic mastermind in a fez. Here, I'm convinced, the obsession begins. This was my first glimpse of the headgear without equal for mystic power. Here, my obsessions with fezzerie begins.

Adding to the strangeness is the ventriloquist routine where Maria sits back to back with her master and speaks his words exactly, like a living puppet. A deep male voice issues from the beautiful female mouth, further complicating the switcheroo master-slave dynamic.

Though a pale-skinned Englishman, Peter Sellers plays an Italian criminal, who further on in the film pretends to be a film director. More convincing, if a far easier role, is Victor Mature's portrayal of a brainless has-been American movie star. He struts and poses, grinning like a good natured shark. A former handsome muscleman (Samson to Hedy Lamar's Delilah) Mature had no delusions of talent and does a charming parody of his beefcake self.

Taken all together, *After the Fox* was the strongest dose of shifting identities I'd ever seen. It also formed in my brain the connections between mysterious Egyptians, sex appeal, criminal capers, and the fez.

Headgear is not mere decoration or protection, not just symbolic or goofball japery. What one wears on the head changes what happens inside that head, that skull, that brain, and its innermost recesses. If William Burroughs could write with his veins full of heroin and wearing a businessman's homburg, if Joseph Smith could experience megalomaniac elation and translate the *Book of Mormon* while staring into a hat with his magic peepstones, then why shouldn't I write this book wearing a fez?

Hakim Bey passed along this factoid about fezzes: the color comes from dye made from *harmel*, which is psychoactive (containing the same chemical as ayahuasca) and is burned as incense to ward off the Evil Eye by heterodox Sufis.

This seemed wistful wishful thinking, another of his implausible discoveries – linking the Moorish fez to hallucinogens. However, with a quick dive into the encyclopedia I found that he was right, not so much intuiting the link as reaching down inside his memory, fishing around, and pulling out something approximating the truth. In fact, an extract from the seeds of Peganum harmala (called wild rue, Syrian rue, African rue or *harmel*) is called Turkey red, and has for centuries been used to dye the traditional Ottoman fez. There is an alkaloid present in the extract which is the same as the main active ingredient in ayahuasca. And yes, the plant is used in Morocco as protection against evil supernatural forces, especially djinn.

Far better than opiates or a gleaming Mormon angel, it was the fez that altered my consciousness.

Refusing acid, cannabis, speed, and jimson weed, I opted for some arcane headgear and began to see through the veil of illusion.

Don the British banker's bowler and your brain is forever different. Put on a World War One doughboy's helmet (I have my grandfather's), a bishop's miter, a pirate's sweat-soaked kerchief, a Stetson, the fur busby of the Death's Head Hussar, a kepi, the Amish woman's well-starched sin-strainer headcovering, a top hat á la Mandrake the Magician and Fred Astaire, a fedora like Bogart, a porkpie as Lester Young wore, or a Spaghetti Western sombrero. Whatever the headgear, visions and visitations are sure to follow.

Some books are created while the author is totally bourbon-drunk or dosed with Benzedrine. Faulkner and Kerouac come to mind. Some are written in alternating states of ecstasy and utter dejection (e.g.: *The Book of Psalms* — happy happy happy — sad sad sad.) Some are the products of diseased minds (Nietzsche, de Sade, Winston Churchill.)

I am writing now in a black fez, with the tassel tickling my left ear. It is my hope, my intention, my solemn vow, to set down the truth while wearing the simple black felt headgear most often associated with middle-aged men zipping around in little cars, with mummy movies, and with hyper-cool Moorish Nobles.

Try this thought experiment: consider writing a symphony while wearing a football helmet. Imagine what kind of banal idiot atrocity would result. Picture this scene: attempting to craft a tender love ballad while wearing a Prussian pickelhaube (with glittering spike and gleaming visor.) A sonnet in a shako? Your first State of the Union speech in a propeller beanie? Fan mail for a beardless boyband in a nun's wimple? The results are obvious and highly unpleasant to contemplate.

In my most exalted states, I wear the Spectral Fez: invisible, ineffable, impossible. Like the literal physical fez, it is a truncated cone, or flat-topped tapering cylinder. But it is also my cerebral cortex augmentation prosthesis — adding another seven inches to my head, making a hollow black skull-extension.

68

TAZ

From his apartment in Crackopolis, Hakim Bey moved to Alphabet City, on Manhattan's Lower East Side. A huge black enforcer patrolled the street, which was totally controlled by drug dealers and who kept the block devoid of any crime. No furtive white men were allowed to stand around on his turf. The mega-goon told me I had to keep moving, and I obeyed.

Hakim Bey had given me instructions: I was to call from the pay phone on the corner and he'd look out the window. I did as I was told, he wrapped the key in a wadded old dirty sock and tossed it down from the fifth floor window. I scurried to retrieve the key, opened the door, and went up five flights of steps to his cold water flat with the bathtub in the kitchen, filled to overflowing with books. Bathing, it was manifestly apparent, came far below reading on his list of priorities.

We drank ridiculously expensive Chinese tea, supposedly of an exquisite nature. The only flavor I could detect was that of the unwashed bowls (with a hint of cigarette ash.) We talked, or I should say, I listened to him talk. Then we repaired to an artsy club called Gargoyle Mechanique. These were the days soon after *Temporary Autonomous Zone* had been published by Autonomedia and was sending ripples through the anarchist zinester world.

His status as a literary shamanic wiseman was then nearing its peak. Walking across Tompkins Square Park, we saw a girl with a T-shirt that said *Hakim's Baby*, with an arrow pointing to her distended stomach. This, given his sexual preferences, caused us both to shudder and smile.

We repaired to the club for some kind of dreary poseur art opening. Afterward, we adjourned downstairs and hung out in the dank, smoky basement. A gaggle of hipster twenty year olds literally sat at Hakim Bey's feet, partaking from the fount of his TAZ wisdom.

The key to his notoriety was the Temporary Autonomous Zone: an uprising which does not engage directly with the state, a guerilla operation which liberates an area (of land, of time, of imagination) and then dissolves itself to reform elsewhere and elsewhen, before the state can crush it. The crucial element of the TAZ was the T. Autonomy was the aspiration of countless groups and movements. And zones were merely areas or regions distinct from others. But the T – for temporary – that was what made the difference. The TAZ ended. It was finite in time, fleeting (and sometimes as ill-remembered) as a dream. With no longevity, it could not ossify into a social fossil with rules, regulations, rigidly established leadership, or long term goals. A TAZ was born, it flourished, and it disappeared.

The essay starts with a flourish sure to attract wannabe tazzers, praising sea rovers and corsairs, wanders briefly into so-called pirate utopias and then gives a tip o' the fez to medieval Assassins. There's plenty of wearisome theory-speak, with then-obligatory references to rapidly deflating gas-bags Baudrillard and Foucault. These passages, I suspect, most readers skipped. Far more appealing was the call for breakthroughs into more intense and more abundant life in the borderland between chaos and order, the margin, the area of catastrophe where the collapse of the system can equal enlightenment. He celebrates small, self-created half-serious / half-fun cults and declares that the primordial-shamanic spirit of the TAZ will usher in an intensification and excess, a potlatch: life spending itself in living. As a model for this phenomenon, he offers the festival or party: genuinely face-to-face. Off the grid, off line, in the flesh — in Hakim Bey's vision, this authenticity was essential. In such fleeting moments, a group of humans combine their efforts to realize mutual desires, whether for good food and cheer, dance, conversation, to create a communal artwork, perhaps even for erotic pleasure.

The 52 page manuscript has a subtitle not found in the published version: *THE TEMPORARY AUTONOMOUS ZONE — or — the pleasures of disappearance.* This document, signed and marked with Hakim Bey's mystic sigil, is still in my possession.

PIRATES

Though he ventured into the then-hip wilds of Cyber-Punk and dreamed of high tech Islands in the Net, in fact Hakim Bey's work was grounded in the mythic past. The first words of *TAZ* evoke a nostalgia for boys' adventure novels and swashbuckler movies. It's fitting that his book about pirate utopias, Moorish corsairs and European renegadoes is made up largely of other people's work. The reader can almost see the tape, staples, and streaks of dried glue stick holding the book together.

It is even more fitting that all of his works bear this statement: *Anticopyright [date.] May be freely pirated and quoted.* This, not his fleeting secret societies or critical theory analysis, was his truly revolutionary act. His words were his most precious treasure and he gave them away, freely, consciously, and with true enjoyment. What other writer has shown such liberty of spirit? None that I'm aware of.

Hakim Bey was a literary buccaneer, with boats made of paper and cannonades of words, not hot iron. His followers were not wolfangels nor seafaring Hawks of the Sea, but pirates of all signs and meanings. In the first paragraph of *TAZ* he places pirates at center stage, yet he laid siege to no Carribean citadels nor led any wild boys to grapple with treasure ships and storm aboard with cutlasses swinging and screams of prepubescent delight.

Pirates, apostates, traitors, degenerates, heretics – what positive meaning could possibly be expected to emerge from such a dire combination? Perhaps none, he admitted, and then considered that he might simply confess to a fascination with the perverse.

In another moment of self-disclosure, he said that piracy is of course despicable – and at the same time a bit romantic. For him, pirates – especially renegadoes, those who'd turned Turke (as the old expression went) and abandoned Christianity – were emblems of resistance and insurrection. Their apostasy manifested the positive shadow of Islam embedded secretly in Christianity. Theirs was a life of indolence and imaginal adventures, not sweat-soaked labor or bloody combat. Piracy could even be viewed as an extreme case of the zerowork ideal. Six months lolling around the Moorish cafes, then a summer cruise on a nice blue ocean, a few hours of manly piratical exertion, and another year of idleness has been financed. Like gangsters in old movies, they thought that work is for saps, and used every expedient to avoid it. An even more grandiose fantasy conceived pirates' murderous greed as a kind of individualist-anarchist desire.

When not rotting in dungeons or hanging on wharf-side gibbets, pirates were free. Vanishing off the map into the ocean mists, they might have enjoyed pure autonomy and perfect sovereignty. Hakim Bey quoted one actual pirate who scorned the king's pardon. "When should I obey a king's orders when I am a kind of king myself?" And he admired another renegado who declared, "I am a free prince."

One such paragon of autonmony was The Sea Hawk (*Sakr – el – Bahr* in Arabic): an Englishman who'd gone Moorish. Until he came up in conversation, I hadn't known that Hakim Bey and I shared a love for the works of Rafael Sabatini. Now largely forgotten, he was a master of the high seas adventure romance. Of all his novels, *Captain Blood* reached the biggest audience. Going through my pirate phase as a young teenager, it was one of my favorites. Later, I saw the big budget film version: Errol Flynn's first swashbuckler.

Less well known (though it too was snatched up by Hollywood) is *The Sea Hawk*. Captain Peter Blood is an Englishman transported to Jamaica as a white plantation slave. He escapes, of course, and sets out to pillage the Spanish Main and gain the love of lovely lady Arabella. The Hawk of the Sea is an English lord who is kidnapped, made a slave on a Moorish galley, then fights his way to dominance as a Moslem corsair captain. With his skin darkened by the sun, wearing a forked beard and turban, he rises quickly within the Basha's lieutenants to become the most feared of the Barbary or Moorish pirates.

Does this Cornish lord become a true follower of Mohammad, or is it all a revenge-fueled sham to wrest back what had been stolen from him in Cornwall? That is one of the puzzles which drives the story forward. What, in 1915 when *The Sea Hawk* was published, did it mean in the English-speaking world to be a true Moslem? What did it mean two years before, when Noble Drew Ali established the Canaanite Temple in Newark, New Jersey?

The corsair swears by Allah, reveres "Our Lord Mahomet," and speaks nothing but praise for the Koran, "the Most Perspicuous Book." He serves and honors the Basha of Algiers and heaps loot at his feet. Yet the Sea Hawk is at heart an Englishman. There were of course others – actual adventurers — who played at this same game. Sir Richard Burton and Lawrence of Arabia top the list. Muhammad Marmaduke Pickthall, whose translation of the Quran loomed over all others for decades, made a public statement of conversion in 1917. And *The Sheik* (novel and film) appeared only a few years later, inducing swoons in millions of English-speaking women.

The Sea Hawk becomes a Moor though, not an Arab. Once he fights his way free of the galley slave's bench on a Spanish ship, he starts anew in the northwest of Africa, home of the Barbary pirates.

"Hell," he tells a fellow slave, observing the odious Catholic priest who is traveling on the Spanish galley, "was surely made for Christians, which may be why they seek to make earth like it." Questioned by his bench-mate, he says, "I renounce from this hour. I am done with Christians and Christianity." Though his conversion to "the Faith of Mahomet" is – as Sabatini tells the reader – superficial, still he is "received into the ranks of the Faithful whose pavilions wait them in Paradise, set in an orchard of never-failing fruit, among rivers of milk, of wine, and of clarified honey." To call his conversion superficial is questionable, as "he embraced the Religion of Mahomet with a measure of fierce conviction."

Likewise, his body is converted. In his half year as a galley slave, side by side with his Moorish friend, "his thews and sinews grew to be equal to their relentless task." In those six months, he becomes "a man of steel and iron, impervious to fatigue, superhuman almost in his endurance." All of this decades before Kal-El came to Earth from Krypton and put on the red, white, and blue tights.

Near the end of the book, facing death at the hands of an English tribunal, the Sea Hawk is asked by a fellow prisoner if he believes in God. He replies, "There is no God but God, and Mohammed is his prophet." In short, he has transformed himself, soul and body, as all great heroes must.

LUDDITES

Besides piratical fantasies, esoteric anarchism, Moorish Mail-order Mysticism, and the daily labor of blackening pages, there was one more crucial point of connection between us. In our own ways – imperfect at best – we were both unrepentant Luddites. My definition is simple: all new technologies are guilty until proven innocent. Hakim Bey's was somewhat more complex. He exhorted his readers to use only technology that would not injure the communality, nothing that replaces human contact and connection. In one of his letters, written in a beautiful calligraphic hand, he told me that our mission should be to exclude as much high tech and mediated reality as possible – to become idyllic pastoral temporary neolithic conservatives – to actually occupy nature.

I attended three Luddite congresses in rural southern Ohio, enjoying the company of other big-hearted nay-sayers. I subscribed to, and wrote for, *Plain*, a magazine (typeset by hand) that gave gentle voice to the resistance. I refused to own a TV, microwave oven, dishwasher, and cell phone, though with great sadness I capitulated and went with internet at home in order to keep my job. The day I signed up for my first email account I flopped on the bed, and wept hot copious tears of shame.

Hakim Bey was the last person I knew who kept up the good fight against cyber-slavery, never learning to use a computer – let alone own one. Now and then he ruminated on the time period in which he'd have preferred to spend his life. The year 1911 came up most often. Film, Victrolas, iceboxes, and phones were available then, but only the most exotic and elegant cars. No radio, no TV, no sea of microwaves churning around our brains, no hyper-real technopathocracy.

He told me there weren't many people in his life with cars and also the desire to go digging into history with a similar view of what they were looking at. That is: a view similar to his. So, he told me repeatedly, my visits were always welcome – and even eagerly anticipated.

I arrived one night and found his house lit only by a few candles. Coming in, I asked if there'd been a power outage. He shrugged, unsure. When I asked if he'd tried the circuit breaker box, again I got a vague response. He was enjoying the absence of electrical light. I found the breaker box, flipped a few switches, and the house came back to life – lamps, fridge, electric heater. Though he acquiesced to this resurgence of techno-power, he told me how much he enjoyed real black-outs, free for a few hours from the noxious hum and buzz of the electrical grid. Living by lamplight, he mused, allowed a person to enjoy the strength and silky texture of a million years of organic life.

Likewise he had no desire to have a working vacuum cleaner. I tried his once, a canister model with rusty Buck Rogers space ship fins. He told me not to bother because he couldn't get it to work. I asked if he'd emptied the chamber where the dust and detritus collected and got a bemused I-don't-know smile, as though it had never occurred to him to attend to such a banal task. I think that in his imaginal realm, the sucked-up dirt somehow instantly disappeared. It wasn't that he couldn't or wouldn't understand how household appliances worked, it was just that there was always something more interesting to think about.

Though hardly an outdoorsman, Hakim Bey related to the natural world (which he called America's most authentic church) in ways that caused me both envy and admiration. I would never live in such squalor, but after spending weekends in his damp, dirty, smoke-filled homes, I drove away feeling oddly rejuvenated.

He called himself a negative Luddite. He didn't have a car or TV or PC or CD player, but he was far from self-sufficient. No garden, no chopping wood, no spinning wheel or hand loom. He shrugged off the critique he faced as a self-styled suburban Luddite and even once let slip the surmise that perhaps it was only the technologies he knew as a boy that he approved of. Everything which appeared after that was threat to his happiness. He was clear about the things he hated: the myriad miseries and alienation of modern life.

The Hun T'un Hermitage was built into the side of a hill. He had one of his anarcho-pothead followers create bathing facilities: half manmade shower stall, half raw bedrock. The next house — in New Paltz — was right on the bank of the Wallkill River, which flooded every year. Running along the side of his last house, in Woodstock, was a stream, and he told me more than once he loved not just the sound but the presence too of living water. It may have been impossible for us to become innocent and primitive — to bomb ourselves back to the stone age, as he put it — but it wasn't impossible to fall in love with what he called the beauty of the earth as a sign of divinity.

Being a Luddite doesn't require slovenly living conditions. Brooms and mops and window screens are old and innocent technologies. For Hakim Bey, cleanliness was simply never a high priority. His stovetop was crusted with glistening black ichor and spent matches. His bathtub and sinks drained with a swampy langour. In the bathroom was a small countertop. There, splayed out with a cracked spine, gummed with cobwebs, was a cheap paperback bio of Queen Victoria. Over the years, I noticed that the browning pages were never turned. So, on every visit, I surreptitiously wrote the date in the margins, up and down the sides, across the top and crammed into the bottom. Finally, when there was no more room to write dates, I asked about the book. It was a random choice from his mountains of reading material. With a shrug and the faintest unembarrassed smile, he said it was for guests to look at while on the toilet.

I put him in contact with my Luddite friends in Ohio and he wrote to thank me for the copies of *Plain* I sent him. He had contacted the editor and sent five dollars for a copy of the *Luddite Journal*. Again, he was just the slightest bit apologetic for being at best a suburban Luddite. Farming was something he'd always been glad other people did. And as for homesteading crafts – he didn't bother to try. He could barely get a new ribbon into his typewriter. The prepubescent boy in him came out when he told me that it was the machine-smashing part of Luddism he liked best. My mention of cell phone towers hidden inside of church steeples triggered in him a fantasy of being young again and well supplied with explosives.

He would call and I'd answer on a 1971 baby blue wall-mounted rotary phone. That is the instrument I use for communicating with the past. Decades later, the sound is still perfect, though only when I connect with another unrepentant Luddite who has hung onto his land line and well-made archaic phone.

Discussing ways to escape the hellscape of the twenty-first century, he said he was sure there was no way to live Luddite on one's own except as a survivalist, which we agreed was a hateful idea. In order to make it a positive experience one needs community. This is the secret – in plain sight — of the Plain People.

He sent these few lines from a recent poem that he thought might amuse me:

> & who am I – this mask that addresses you but leaves no address – this message in a bottle?
> In the scene where angry peasants with torches
> Storm the lightning-crowned mad doctor's lab
> Screaming Down With Progress or Smash the Machines
> I'm there in the mob – face hidden in a cowl
> Hunched & lumpen – shaking misshapen fist
> With Epimethean rancor at the burning keep.

Sharing my grief at what the editor of *Plain* called the "sheer physical ugliness of the modern world," Hakim Bey wrote to me a challenge. It sounded to him as though I'd have to do something soon about my plain tendencies or else begin to suffer too much. He left me with this question: how far would I have to go before I hit the 19th century?

VISITATIONS

The original incarnation of the MOC owned land in Herkimer County. One draw was the nearness of Stone Arabia, a town with the hippest possible Moorish name and postal address. Sadly though, with no building for long term lodging, and a good hundred miles from the main Moorish concentration, the land was seldom used as an ashram, and was eventually sold. Until the effluoresence of the Ziggurat Lodge, this was the farthest into New York State that the MOC had reached.

Sometimes, the mid-sixties Church forayed undercover as a motorcycle club – the MOC-MC. Hakim Bey had a tricycle, he told me with nostalgic pride. No license, three wheels, and a powerful motor. Though implausible, yet I can picture him on a roaring triune road-god. Helmet decorated with Arabic symbols? Fez? Turban? Or wild hippie freak-flag hair whipping in the wind? Any of these are perfect.

Decades later, when the MOC was again extending its ectoplasmic tentacles into the soft white underbelly of New York State, I'd travel a half dozen hours and spend the weekend with Hakim Bey. Often on my trips downstate, we'd take a long afternoon jaunt, hunting up traces of what was or what might've been.

In all but a few cases, we found no tottering ruins nor arcane hillside carvings to admire.

Sometimes it would merely be for good food: excellent pastrami in a tiny Catskill deli or a slab of fine pork from the Metzgerei (a German butcher shop between Woodstock and Saugerties.) The grand Hudson highlands, the Catskill peaks, abandoned canals, the hilltop estate of self-satisfied millionaire hippies, or haggling with a Persian rug merchant: we scouted and scoured Hakim Bey's territory.

On one long hike in a state park, we came to the cave (really no more than a rock overhang) that might've been the hideout of a legendary bandit. This wasn't entirely make-believe. We'd done our due diligence, poring over the meager records of 19th century renegadoes. From Washington Irving's literary legends to the work of fine local historian Alf Evers, Hakim Bey read all he could to discover clues and remnants of past bizarreries.

We stopped at a town where witchcraft was said to have flourished, poked around and found nothing of note. A number of other nearby towns had been flooded and were now fathoms below the reservoirs created to provide New York City with water. We peered into the depths, hoping to see a ghostly steeple poking up from the murk. Hakim Bey had a friend who oversaw in some obscure manner what remained of the Widow Jane iron mine. We went a short distance in. It was mostly flooded, a cave with a black lake or tarn, as Edgar Allen Poe would've called it. After my companions had left, I stood on the inky shore to sing a tune that had been current back when miners hewed out the living rock. "Do not I love thee dearest Lord? Behold my heart and see." The echoes were wonderful, coming back to me like the voices of long-dead, long-forgotten men.

We climbed a steep hillside to reach the Prattsville Rocks – strange, huge, primitive carvings of a horse and a disembodied arm swinging a hammer, like a crude New York State Mt. Rushmore. We tracked down the Yellow Church, one of the only remnants of the Primitive (or so-called hardshell) Baptists in the region. The building was pleasant enough, but unremarkable, only used twice a year for religious gatherings. But it was of the same denomination that had preserved the much-beloved nineteenth century hymns in the *Sacred Harp*. I discovered, up front in the pulpit, a hymnal of the same lineage, and in that hymnal I found the song I'd sung in the Widow Jane mine.

His charm coming through in these situations, Hakim Bey would phone to find out if we could get inside a lost/found site, and the answer was often a sweet yes. There always seemed to be two old history ladies serving as genteel sentinels for places like this, and my guide was highly skilled at getting the goods from them, whether the key to a secret door or some tidbit of local lore. In this case, the history ladies told us we had to go out to the church's cemetery to see their most notable gravestone. This took a bit of wandering, but we did indeed find the marker, which told of a boy "spurred to death by a rooster."

Hakim Bey described our journeys as thaumaturgic pyschogeography — deliberate re-enchantment of landscape – archeo-emotional rescue of spatial meaning. But at his best he didn't need grand-sounding tongue twisters. On these trips into backwards time and sideways space, the evidence we found was often scanty or of questionable authenticity. To truly enter these realms, we depended on something far more potent than academic theory or flavor-of-the month ideologies.

Great historians are sorcerers, summoning the past in the fleeting flicker of the present. I make no claims to such exalted status. And few readers, even his most devoted followers, would say that Hakim Bey was a great historian. Disdaining academic plodding, fast and loose with the so-called facts, he created, he conjured the past rather than merely making tiresome piles of verifiable evidence. History, after all, is a game. The point is to be the knights – not pawns. We devoted ourselves to the history of images and ideas, which shape human society whether or not they are based in so-called historical reality.

Our trip to Pollepel Island discovered nothing new or useful for historians. If anything, my understanding of this place was more muddy, rather than clearer, after we'd wandered the ruins there. Yet our day was overripe with meaning, a mini-voyage into the mythic past.

If you take the train from western New York State to New York City (which I've done many times) it heads south at Albany and in Hakim Bey's region follows the banks of the Hudson River for miles. Truly beautiful in places, this leg of the journey was always my favorite. Here, passengers like me passed the famous Highland features captured again and again by painters of the Hudson River School. Romanticized in art and literature, the region has none of the grandeur of the Rockies, or even the Adirondacks. Yet it has rich history — false, true, and neither.

The tracks run along the bed of the old New York Central, the railroad that did more than any to help create New York City. Here the Twentieth Century Limited, America's most famously elegant and most celebrated passenger train, ran from 1902 until 1967. And as the cars roared past Pollepel Island, travelers peered out for a glimpse of crumbling walls and tottering towers.

Pollepel Island lies about a quarter mile off the east bank of the Hudson. There are flats of shallow water both north and south, but a channel deep enough for steam tugs flows between the island and the mainland. What makes it noteworthy is Bannermans Castle — five stories tall, absurdly ornate, with columns, a grand stairway, crenelated turret tops and over a hundred windows, long open to the wind, rain, snow, and flocking birds.

Francis Bannerman grew rich as a war profiteer, beginning in 1865 when at age fourteen he bought up surplus arms at auction. He continued to trade in arms and ammunition for decades. He had been storing his vast stocks of war materiel in New York City, but a municipal law forced him to locate his arsenal elsewhere. He bought Pollepel island in 1900 and began the creation of his personal estate and ammo dump in 1905. He was still working on the castle at his death in 1918.

It was supposed to evoke the baronial estates of his native Scotland, but even in its early, intact, state it looked more like an overloaded Italian wedding cake than the castle of a proud laird. In 1920 an explosion blew a twenty-five foot hole in one wall and brought down a turret. The family continued to use the castle as a storehouse until 1967, when they sold the island to the State of New York.

When we ventured to the island by boat, it was still relatively safe to wander the ruins. No guns, bayonets, artillery shells or helmets remained. Most had been sold or given away. The rest were picked over decades before we arrived to explore the island. Huge slabs of concrete and stone had fallen, flooded cellars yawned beneath the tangles of weeds, the castle devolving back into the rock it was built on. My guide had done his reading in local lore, which added to the mystique of our jaunt.

Indians believed the island was haunted and wouldn't spend the night here. Early Dutch mariners believed it was the northern boundary of the Dunderberg goblins' domain. Sailors new to the Hudson were inoculated against the Heer of Dunderberg (a mythological thunder-lord) by being ducked into the river as the boats passed the island.

What did I learn that day? Not much. What did I feel? Some sadness (knowing that I'd never again wander the stony seven acre island), some delight in the power of the elements to grind down human follies, and some wonder. No goblins or ghosts remained, as far as I knew. But still the place was haunted. Obscure lore, charming tales, secret landscapes, tunnels to nowhere, abandoned buildings – these are all abodes of the still-living dead.

There's no evidence that Francis Bannerman was anything but a vicious war profiteer with bad taste in architecture. Of his family, I learned nothing. Yet he did bequeath to me something to look forward to as my train rumbled beneath the Hudson Highlands. And for one day, with Hakim Bey, I could wander the ruined memorial he'd raised to his own ego, his now long-forgotten importance.

TIME OFF

I took it as a great compliment when he said I was probably the only contemporary writer whose Collected Letters he'd like to read. Of course this isn't saying much, because I was the only contemporary writer he knew who actually wrote real letters.

He never wavered in his effusive praise for the post: *handwritten, private, mysterious, brought to your very door by an unseen hand for only pennies per message, the money having been transformed into beautiful stamps. Please! Write long letters! Let's start a movement!*

From there, he went again into his fantasy of escaping to a medieval monastery. He'd just received the newsletter of Holy Cross Monks (not far from Woodstock) and went through his usual half hour of teeth-gnashing envy, thinking about those Anglican Friar Tucks tucking into their Benedictine victuals and lolling about amongst the incense and Gregorian chant.

Indolence, he told me more than once, is both a virtue and a human right. Off-handedly, he called himself an unemployed uninsured slugabed. Depending on his mood, he either embraced wholeheartedly his economic uselessness, or shrugged it off as a minor irrelevance.

Reclining on a carpet, smoking and drinking tea, he soliloquized about his wish to be part of a community, not a dour post-hippie commune, but a society slothful as the Ottomans, wasting the days on tulips and opium mysticism and kite-flying. Not for him the relentless grinding busyness, the deadly cankerous growth that dooms America. Then, with a smile, he gave a tip o' the fez to the Byzantines who debated the sex of Angels even as the walls were falling.

He freely admitted to the good fortune that allowed him his life of indolence and literature. He was the product of the short-lived and perhaps unique leisure society of the '60s. He made the decision to use his good luck (an only child, born into a middle-class family) to opt for free time and cultural pleasures over wage slavery or the quest for success. And he never regretted it, though he was aware that a time might come when he would be broke, sick, and uninsured. As for the Devil Depression, his antidotes were work (his work, thousands of pages) and some self-medication. Half joking, he said that he'd toyed with the idea of having himself judged mentally incompetent (but ambulatory) so he could have a life of pure indolence.

In another letter he sent the following rumination, which he called "Time Off For No Particular Behavior."

The luxury of an empty day can only be compared to the pleasure of an empty head — probably our only hope for any Egyptian immortality — sideways in time — the death-defying slow leap over Niagara, chained to a bear.

We're from the Fortean Society, all we want is just the facts, ma'am, just the mindless jubilation. Or failing that, at least a few empty titles, patents of extinct nobility, admiralties in the salvation navy of a dying creed.

Entheogenic ceremonialism for nietzschean nieces and nephews, the Nth generation, masters of time travel but only in one jerkwater minor alternate dimension. Look — a shack on stilts on pier on bayou amid vast okeefenochian vistas of tannic tarns and funeral moss.

APOCRYPHA

Along with telling me his waking visions, he also — in person and through the mail — passed along certain almost-lost texts which tell of dream time exploration. Contained in one of the 8 ½ by 11 envelopes that appeared in my mail box was a rare and valuable bit of '60s ephemera. This was a copy of *Ustad Selim's Veridical Dream Book*, "printed by the Bolan Muslim Press, Quetta, West Pakistan."

It's only eight pages long, the flimsy cream-yellow paper going brown around the edges, its single staple long gone. If this booklet were a hoax, then it had been done with loving care: hand typeset, full of misaligned words and typos. The copy I received is from "A special Edition of 100." Mine is numbered (by hand) 38, and signed with an Arabic glyph. A reference to another figure who appears in the first incarnation of the *Moorish Science Monitor* ("Dr. Zill has located the dream eye tentatively in the pineal gland") is also intriguing.

Who was the author of this fragile bit of Moorish ephemera (dated 1970)? There are poems attributed to Ustad Selim in the first run of the *Monitor*. Was this an earlier manifestation of Hakim Bey? I'll never know for sure, as he neither denied nor affirmed the identity of Ustad Selim. Different books

— different personae: manifesting himself with various pseudonyms. Scholar, poet, raconteur, critic, pornographer, prophet.

Name-changing is common among the esoteric greats. Timothy Drew became Noble Drew Ali. Plain Joe Smith became Joseph the Mormon Prophet. Sun Ra spent his early years as Herman Blount. Aleister Crowley had at least a half dozen different names and titles, among them Edward Alexander Crowley (at birth), Perdurabo, the Laird of Boleskine, and the Beast 666. Superheroes and supervillains, magicians and spies, have secret identities. There's a great deal of that within the MOC — a sense of illusion and playacting. I'm convinced however that in these real-world cases, it's far more than a mere game. Self-transformation is an obvious reason for this phenomenon. Deeper perhaps is the will or intention. I was that — ordinary. I will become this — extraordinary.

I have five male friends — real friends, not annoying internet phantoms — who've legally changed their names. One hated his father — for good reasons — and took his mother's last name. One was tired of people thinking he was Jewish, so he changed one letter and became echt Deutsch. Another was sick of being a generic New Jersey suburbanite and went back to his forefathers' eastern European, hyper-Jewish, name. A fourth had a name that sounded almost obscene. He was tired of people sniggering when he introduced himself, so once his parents had died, he changed his name to the correct pronunciation in Polish. And a fifth said, "I'm sick of being a loser." So he, like the others, went through the rigmarole to change his name in the eyes of the law, becoming "Winner."

I too have worn a number of self-styled names. I was Mot before I understood that we read left to right. Then Bomber (from Tom the Bomb.) Thom with an H. Thommy 3X (pronounced "Tommy Three Times.") Bodo Aussieht. Lev Bronstein (Leon Trotsky's real name). Ziggurat. Leander Watts. V-Rocket. Blind Dudu Process. Mistah Tawm (singing in Alabama).

These shifting identities hardly make me a mage or wizard. But they do give a glimpse of what it means to shed the banal for the remarkable. As a few honest actors will acknowledge, we often become what we pretend to be.

Another friend, who is proud to say he's never flown under false colors, argues back: "Yeah, but none of it is real."

"You saw my diploma — " which established the Ziggurat Lodge. I'd framed it and hung it in my office.

"You know what I mean," my friend persisted. He'd never met Hakim Bey, though he'd read *Temporary Autonomous Zone* and was both intrigued and repelled. "Wannabe anarchists glommed onto it because he gave them a cool name for what usually was just a drunken party." Something, everything, about the MOC bothered him. "It's not even his real name. And Noble Drew Ali — "

"He was real. There's plenty of evidence." I'd showed him a picture, and some scholarly articles about the Moorish Science Temple. In *Black Gods of the Metropolis,* published in 1944, there's an entire chapter describing the temple in detail.

"Come on. You know what I mean. There are plenty of bullshit flimflam cults." Some have called Noble Drew Ali a clever con man, and he was known at times to take the stage as a magician and escape artist. That didn't, however, make him or Hakim Bey swindlers or frauds. For one thing, neither of them got rich on any of their Moorish schemes.

Yet there was always an element of the imaginal (one of his favorite words) about Hakim Bey's arcane endeavors. "If you mean bullshit as in out and out lies to fool the gullible, then absolutely not. There's not a whiff of the creepy cult leader about him."

I quoted — verbatim — something Hakim Bey had told me. *I'm not really interested in preaching, and I don't think myself a guru in any sense. I'm not interested in establishing some sort of personality cult. I really would like to be invisible.*

"Okay. So he's not a con man. I understand that he's your friend. But it still could be bullshit. I heard somebody say he was like a really smart eleven year old who lived in his own private fantasy worlds. All the research, all the writing, diplomas and secret societies, rites and fezzes . . . Jesus, what is it with you guys and fezzes? All of that could just be fairy tales to avoid reality."

"And what's so great about your so-called reality?" I asked. My friend's accusations were pointed — obliquely — at me too.

"How many fezzes do you have?"

"I don't know. I've lost count."

"Why so many?"

"People give them to me now. They see one cheap in a sale, and know that it'll have a good home, right here." I'd talked my friend into posing in hieratic headgear and gotten a picture of him looking both confused and disdainful of such nonsense.

"You don't believe any of this, right?"

"It's got nothing to do with belief."

My friend had heard me run this idea before: insisting that belief is a useless word, always muddying any discussion. "Doctrine and dogma, canons and creeds: that's the real bullshit."

Hakim Bey said it far more elegantly, describing texts which exist in the intersection of real and unreal, authorized and forbidden.

The world of apocrypha is a world of books made real. The apocryphal imagination turns "Tibet" or "Egypt" into amulets or mantram with which to unlock an "other world," most real in books and dreams and dreams of books.

In the world of apocrypha the images of established religion and canonical texts acquire a kind of mutability, a tendency to drift, so that the texts become fluid organic mosaics with replaceable parts, each bit catching and reflecting a shard of light, like a magpie's hoard. This is not plagiarism in the crude sense of the word, as the texts themselves take on a certain autonomy, a nomadic life of their own. And thus are born the scriptures of heresies, the canons of the gnostics, the rants of the cults of love and light.

ANARCHO-MONARCHISM

With each new letter, it seemed, he founded a new imaginal movement. Next was *Irrealism – a step beyond surrealism.* It would, he claimed, serve as an umbrella for all his movements – Endarkenment, Escapism, Impossibilism, Suburban Luddism, Phlogiston Theory, Neptunism, Hollow Earth, the Cro-Magnon Liberation Front. And he of course suggested that I join up.

In my next letter, I told him that I'd be happy to join. All that meant was that I wanted to hear more about his latest foray into wit and weirdness. But by the time he received my assent and replied, he'd wandered down another imaginal pathway.

I had described the investigations I was making into the life of my shadowy Scottish great-grandfather, Walter Mercel: starting off as a coal miner, moving out of the pit as a stationary engineer, moving to Canada, and then the U.S., and retiring quite well off as the Bertillon expert at the Monroe County Jail.

The response I received was a tangle of genealogy, lost history, and magic lore. I wouldn't hear any arguments from Hakim Bey against immersing myself in the ancestral vortex. He'd been doing it himself ever since childhood, with Scottish legends and the Irish Twilight, and especially since his first visit to Ireland in 1991. More recently he'd joined the Stewart Society and was in touch with a Polish count who called himself the legitimate pretender to the Throne of Scotland. He'd also discovered – or perhaps dreamed – that he was descended from Francis Stewart, Fifth Earl of Bothwell – the notorious warlock who tried to assassinate King James VI/I by raising a storm at sea to drown him (Halloween 1590) – but the black cat escaped and the spell fizzled.

Hakim Bey is best known for his anarchist writings. Yet no matter how hard others may have tried (and will continue to do so), it's impossible to jam him into a neat ideological pidgeon hole. Regarding Celtic nobility, he exhorted me to find the hidden aspects – the secret rebel traditions and the sad beauty — and just ignore reality.

He remain fixated on childhood obsessions such as piracy and Celtic Nationalism. Over the course of his life he'd accrued such a crazy-quilt of notions that the contradictions sometimes overwhelmed the revelations. He'd been an anarchist since he was twelve years old, but he also always had a romantic Jacobitish penchant for decadent monarchies. His solution to these conundra was to declare himself an ambulatory schizophrenic and to hold all his ideas at the same time – and to syncretize them, to write them into existence. One of the products of this both/and thinking was another movement: Anarcho-Monarchism.

Literally anarchy means no rulers, and monarchy is the rule by one supreme person. But oxymorons were no impediment to his imagination and poetry. In the world of the irrational, all is possible, or at least conceivable. In the imaginal realm (the *mundus imaginalis,* a term he borrowed from Henry Corbin, the great scholar of Sufism) the rules of the so-called waking world are suspended. In sleep he dreamed of only two forms of government – anarchy and monarchy, only kings and and wild people populated his night. In dreams he was never ruled except by love or sorcery.

He understood the objections that doctrinaire anarchists were sure to pose. Yet he managed to forge a link between two seemingly opposite impulses. The single absolute ruler acts as a mirror for the unique and utter absoluteness of the self. Already, he promised, we were the monarchs of our own skin. Our inviolable freedom waited to be completed only by the love of other monarchs.

If you had known the sweetness of life as a poet in the reign of some venal, corrupt, decadent, ineffective and ridiculous Pasha or Emir, some King Farouk, some Queen of Persia, you would know that this is what every anarchist must want. How they loved poems, those dead luxurious fools. Hate their cruelty and caprice, yes – but at least they were human. And besides: the dreamer, the artist, the anarchist – do they not share some tinge of cruel caprice with the most outrageous of moghuls?

LOST / FOUND

When we met, he flung the titles of books, the names of thinkers and writers, at me like rice at a wedding, a fertility rite of the mind. It was through him that I first encountered Islamic anarchism, Siberian shamanism, the utopian fantasies of Charles Fourier, the failed sex experiments of Sar Peladan, James Hogg (the Ettrick Shepherd), obscure Persian poets, Erasmus (not Charles) Darwin, Hermes Trismegistus, Taoist ancestor possession, and the Donald Duck comics of Carl Barks.

Neither *Semiotext(e) USA* nor the *SF* anthology contains my best work, but there I was, a young writer among some greats. The *Gone to Croatan* anthology had a far stronger impact on me. Subtitled, "Origins of North American Dropout Culture," it contains some groundbreaking pieces. And my contribution was also my first real work of renegado scholarship. I called it "Transform and Rebel." That said it all. One must become something new and different, something rich and strange (even if it's fakery, or patently ridiculous), in order to break the shackles of the mind.

My article was about the Calico Indians, a fine example of high weirdness and cross-ethnic / cross-gender transgression. These so-called Indians had hoods and gowns made of frontier calico, in order to keep their identities hidden as they fought against the oppressive power of their patroons (New York State's original feudal lords.) This was in former Mohawk territory, and yet the disguises look less like Mohawk costumes than like a feminized KKK gown. I examined one of these at the state museum in Kingston, pulled from storage and wrapped in acid-free tissue paper. As with so much of so-called history, this was probably a fake. To escape reprisals, the real Calico Indians had buried and burned their get-ups once their rebellion had been extinguished. Yet the gown and hood still gave a glimpse of what had likely happened, as did my trip to Delhi, where some of the Calico Indians had been held prisoner. Nothing of the jail remained in Delhi, but like so many of these jaunts into the multi-layered past, some research and the spell of imagination coaxed out of the shadows a time when things now called impossible were thought to be real — and even crucial.

I did the research and had the story, but as I'd never written an article of this nature before, I was unsure how to proceed. Though I'd published numerous stories and novels, at that point I needed a model. So, I read again "Lost/Found Moorish Time Lines" and broke it down paragraph by paragraph.

I used the structure, though for a completely different factual story. My model's first line: "The image: crumbling 1920s photograph of an American black man dressed in robe, sash, and fez, posing formally hand on breast like Napoleon, labeled 'Prophet Noble Drew Ali 1886-1929.'" My first line: "The remains: a costume and mask stored behind glass like a saint's garments in a reliquary."

I thought of this not as mere imitation, but like a jazz musician building new tunes on old chord changes. ("I Got Rhythm," for instance, is the foundation of dozens of compositions, from "Anthropology" and "Lester Leaps In" to the Flintstones' theme.)

My article first appeared in *Anarchy: A Journal of Desire Armed*. But it had been commissioned for *Gone to Croatan* and was published there in book form. This anthology brought together a remarkable mixture of scholarship, biographical writing, poetry, and flights of fancy. Talking with Hakim Bey and the editors about the project brought into the light the beauty of the cultural mishmash. In particular, *Gone to Croatan* focused on tri-racial isolates. These groups were small and secretive (in some cases legendary), whose ancestors were American Indians, escaped or freed slaves, and whites who'd dropped out of colonial America and gone into the wilderness. Intermarrying, the three racial strains were tangled and blurred until they fit into no standard category. Usually, these groups were given absurd names (e.g.: Jukes, Nams, Jackson Whites) and seen as cacogenic. That is, they were supposedly polluted with noxious genes, and thus were deserving of extermination.

Harpocrates Ben Ishmael Bey sent me a bibliography of works that he'd been studying. This document is twenty-four pages long, hand-written, folded and side-stapled, a precious one-of-a-kind booklet that opened up numerous shadowy avenues for research.

Out of this came my interest in eugenics and racism, and my article "Vicious Protoplasm: Eugenics and Modern Sex War." My novel, *Drowning in Fire* (the original hoodooistic title — *The Mandrake Hand* — was rejected by the editor), is a sex-and-crime thriller with tri-racial isolates in the murky background. Kush, the old man in a fez, is to a certain degree based on Hakim Bey. Research for the novel sent me into the swamps of south Jersey, and to the mental hospital where some of the last victims of eugenic sterilization were kept incarcerated. As an epigraph, I used a line from Hakim Bey's *Chaos*: "I am awake only in what I love and desire to the point of terror."

ALCHEMY OF THE WORD

He admitted to being a lifelong print addict, and I shared with him some of the same obsessive relationship to the written word. William Burroughs famously said that language is a virus. As a lifelong junkie, he might more plausibly have said that language acts as a drug. Stacks of books, drifts of pamphlets, scrolls and sigils, graffiti and grimoires, words carved into a school desk, weighty esoteric tomes, the speech balloons in comic books, gravestone epitaphs dissolving in acid rain, subtitles in Samurai films, dyslexic Tijuana Bibles, greasy menus listing obscure delights: all of these have the potential to intoxicate.

Seen at a certain oblique angle, Hakim Bey was a man made out of words, a story telling itself. Whether it was the multi-hour private monologues I soaked up, his radio broadcasts wafting through the luminiferous aether, or the countless pages he blackened with inky thoughts, language itself was his alchemical instrument.

At times he could turn the perfect phrase. *Poetic terrorism* and *temporary autonomous zone* captured the anarcho-hipster zeitgeist and gained him a modicum of celebrity. Elsewhere he dealt in polysyllabic prolixity and otiose obfuscation. For me, it was the poetry that mattered. Whether in prose or verse, certain of his phrases had (and still have) a sorcerous effect. *The black light of jaguars. Astral travel on February nights. Catskill warlock shrines.* What do these mean? I'm not sure. What is their effect? They cause my mind to buzz, seethe, and throb.

He proclaimed that the acquisition of language falls under the sign of Eros. Forbidden wisdom, blasphemous credos, alchemical formulae, lost and found love poems, rumors, and spells: language itself can be as sensual as its content. Regarding heretical writings, Hakim Bey told me that certain texts are pregnant with unspoken yearning, quite erotic in tone. Words crafted together in esoteric combinations can manifest our desires and our intentions. A poem can act as a spell and vice versa — but his sorcery refuses to be a metaphor for mere literature. It insists that symbols must cause events as well as private epiphanies.

Regarding Rimbaud's alchemy of the word, he said that it offered much promise, yet delivered much disappointment. The text which will change reality: Rimbaud dreamed of that and then gave up in disgust. But he had entertained too subtle an idea about magic, and in fact texts can only change reality when they inspire readers to act, rather than merely see.

Giving up poetry for commerce, Rimbaud became a merchant of obsolete rifles and fine coffee in Abyssinia, and died of cancer. His poems were left behind, inspiration for some and a warning for others, weatherbeaten signs on the road to oblivion. The written word itself may have taken us to the very edge beyond which writing may be impossible. Yet Hakim Bey could still see texts trembling just beyond the veil.

His letters were one of kind and private in a way that digital communication can never be. With weight, tactile texture, scent, and existing in and moving through three dimensions, all letters come from the past. Even with the most perfect postal system, there is always a time lag between the sender and the receiver. And that wait — days, weeks, sometimes months — helps to transform the letter into an amulet, a charm, even a fetish object.

Imagine perfumed letters sealed with red wax and heraldic imagery: letters like Prince Genji used to write, or Proust, who could send little blue notes by pneumatic post anywhere in Paris. Think of mail-order degrees in Rosicrucianism. Yes, the post — under the sign of Hermes — is sheer magic.

In response to one of my questions, he looped back decades, telling the origin story of his gorgeous calligraphic letters.

The key to decent handwriting is a good pen. Mine is an Osmiroid (nice name) — I like the Italic nib. When I was young I had atrocious handwriting — like most Americans — because penmanship was not taught in school. The French used to have good hands — all of them! — because calligraphy was taught in school (I think this is no longer so.) My 7th grade teacher believed that my spelling was poor because I couldn't read my own writing. I began practising, using books on calligraphy as models. I never got to a real professional level, but I do think that "writing" includes handwriting. The only time I ever did typed first drafts was when I worked on a newspaper.

I sent him articles I was writing for the local alt paper, about pet cemeteries, home schooling, teen Jesus jamborees, drag racing, evangelical balloon twisting, and disgusting snack foods.

He replied, *Mein Gott! Your genius is wasted in provincial journalism! Maybe not "to bloom unseen" exactly — but I'm sure the rubes don't deserve you.*

I wrote back to him about a dream of apostolic succession that descended from H. P. Lovecraft. In the dream, there was a stately old wizard who derived his power-and-mystery directly from HPL. And he bestowed it upon me by the use of a syringe full of morphine. He didn't inject me, but squirted the narcotic juice into my nose. I asked for an interpretation.

This came back in postal reply. *The HPL dream — you are the apostolic successor — the morphine in your nose is the passing-on of the flame of inspiration.* Then he mentioned a work in progress, dedicated to me, called "Autism Sonnets," which he'd drafted after our conversation on the subject. Once finalized, he promised, he could send it my way. He never did.

For a time, I was having some modest success writing young adult novels under the pseudonym Leander Watts. His response was to tell me about two fantasy/science fiction novellas he'd written, and then to ask *What to do? Should Hakim Bey sell-out and do "pop" fiction? (If anyone cares.)*

We both understood that collaboration means twice the work and half the money. But he did on occasion float the idea. *You and I should put together a real book of Weird NY — not the cheap ghosts or the usual suspects. Ask your agent if we could get paid for such a book (because if we're going to sell out our secrets we oughta get actually paid.) I have unpublished and unfinished texts on the Newburgh Druids, Hermeticism in Colonial Hudson Valley, Jukes, Pang Yang, etc. Sounds like . . . too much work! What do you reckon?*

Somewhere — on the Astral Plane, in Hyperborea, in Taoist hell — the book was published and garnered rave reviews. However, no royalty payments passed the boundary between the Here and the Hereafter.

GANESH BABA

When the Greenwood Lake cottage became untenable (it was always hard to reach without a car), he moved his operations to a house on the banks of the Wallkill River. Off in the western distance was Mohonk Mountain, a Victorian-era mountaintop resort complete with stone observation tower silhouetted against the sunset sky. I went to this charmingly seedy old hotel only once, to climb the tower's steps and look down, like a young god, on the high altitude lakes.

Within a year, Hakim Bey's new home had taken on much the same dissolute charm as the Hun T'un Hermitage. More dampness, more smoke and mold spoors, unwashed dishes, drifts of manuscripts, and more stacks of books. Soon vines were penetrating right through the walls, as though seeking their seed-home. Poison ivy totally engulfed the front door and it was abandoned. I was forbidden to open the fridge door, for fear something monstrous and nauseating would slither out. On a high shelf was a bottle of genuine Slovenian wormwood, shrouded in cobwebs.

When I visited, I slept on the ground floor, with an electric fan going to keep the bugs off of me. Built, like the Hun-T'un Hermitage, directly into living rock, this lower room was never dry. The books stored there, the Chinese amulets and photos on the walls, curled like ancient scrolls.

In every place he made his home, he displayed the same picture of King Farouk: the patron saint of indolent elegance. In the lower chamber in the house on the Wallkill, there he was, posed in hieratic tuxedo, sash and fez. The last royal ruler of Egypt, Farouk was deposed in 1952, spending the rest of his life (another thirteen years) getting fatter, living a life of glorious self-indulgence in Italy.

Also, wherever Hakim Bey lived, a photo of a tubby smiling sadhu had a place of prominence. It had been snapped in an amusement park and showed this famous dope guru, Ganesh Baba, with an astronaut ride behind him has backdrop.

More than once I was told this story about the roly-poly sadhu.

We were walking in the square one day. He always carried a tightly rolled umbrella as part of his shtick. We were walking along and he stopped to play football with some little kids. They loved it and they loved him. He could make himself accessible to anyone at any moment, including street kids.

Then we walked on a little ways and he suddenly attacked this guy, started beating him over the head with his umbrella. After he chased him away, after beating him over the head and cursing him, I said, "Ganesh, who was that?"

He said, "I don't know."

"Then why were you beating him?"

He said, "I did not like the look of that fellow — a very bad man."

That was all the explanation I ever got. He knew the guy was bad — in fact he looked like a weasel — and deserved to be beaten over the head. He weaseled away. He looked terrified that this hefty — not very tall, but quite plump and hefty — sadhu was attacking him in front of everyone.

In a minute he turned from a cherub playing football with these little street kids into an avenging angel with an umbrella.

BOUNDARY VIOLATIONS

Cops. That was the theme of the next issue of the *Moorish Science Monitor* to make it into my mailbox. Presented by Verlag Golem, its masthead declared itself to be the "delight of the intelligent and for friends the rare gift." A guest editor, Joe Bastard Armpit, set the tone. Also implicated were Ali Hossein ("one-eyed and luckless son of shame"), Sir William Jerkoff, Feral Faun, and Hakim Bey.

This issue went in a new and more scabrous direction. That is, far more queer and far more pornographic. I wasn't ready for these illustrations: motorcycle cops with giant thrusting man-units, handcuffs around scrotums, naked masturbating pretty-boys, and cops kissing the Pope's hand. But I plunged in, sure that something special, crazed, hilarious, filthy, and true would be discovered in these twenty-four xeroxed pages.

In Church News, the Dagon Temple of Providence unveiled its daring defense initiative — the Legion of Religious Heroes. This included such youthful paragons of law and order as Quaker Lass, Zen Kid, Buddha Girl, and Jew Boy. A collage by James Koehnline, a translation from Hesiod and a quote auf deutsch from Nietzsche round out the issue. An excerpt from Hakim Bey's "Crime" gives a good idea what these degenerate Moors were up to.

Don't just survive while waiting for someone's revolution to clear your head. Don't sign up for the armies of anorexia and bulimia. Act as if you were already free. Calculate the odds — step out — remember the Code Duello. Smoke Pot / Eat Chicken / Drink Tea. Every man his own vine and figtree (Circle Seven Koran) — carry your Moorish passport with pride. Don't get caught in the crossfire. Keep your back covered, but take the risk. Dance before you calcify.

With publication in the hands of the mad Verlag Golem crew, the *Monitor* became more overtly anti-authoritarian, sexually provocative, and far more funny, including a call to claim "Sodom for the Sodomites!" What did this have to do with the Moorish Science Temple? Not much, at first and second glance. Noble Drew Ali resisted oppressive authority, but was proud to be an American. Never a dirty, wild-eyed anarchist, he looked absolutely great in feathered turban, embroidered tunic, silk trousers, shiny shoes, and broad brocaded sash.

The word "anarchism" was common — almost a requirement — in the zines I first read. Everyone with a typewriter, scissors, a glue stick, and access to a xerox machine was touting their brand of Circle A revolution. Feral Faun directs his rant, "We Can Be Heroes," to a "small number of heretics, anarchists, chaos magicians and marginals . . . wild and strange

. . . proudly androgynous." Hakim Bey rejected old-line rigid politics and used the words "chaos" and "anarchism" interchangeably. Describing a so-called Moorish pirate utopia, he employed a similar verbal sleight of hand. This much, he whispered, will suffice: it could have been real and it should have been real. Therefore, this hypothetical piratical paradise was a genuine act of spontaneous political genius.

Freedom, wild self-expression, boundary violations, heresy, and mad humor. Would Noble Drew Ali have approved, or even deigned to read such scurrilous screeds? Very unlikely. But he was long dead and the remnant of his religion had mutated into the hard-line scowl of the Black Muslims, not so different from the rigid police character armor that Feral Faun assails in his rant. These new/old words and images were tools for liberation, not scripture or icons.

So was the *Monitor* just a toy for intellectual playtime and make believe, the voice of another joke religion? I didn't think so when I first encountered it and I don't think so years later. It doesn't matter what any of this meant, how true or authentic is was. I cared then and I care now what something does, its consequences in the inner and outer worlds. And gazing into the pages of these mad giveaways had the effect of opening up my mind to new possibilities. The world was a bigger place with each new surreptitious contact.

At the time there were a number of so-called

joke religions manifesting as tracts, zines, crudely-published books, and manifestos snaking through the U.S. Mail. The Church of the SubGenius was probably the most successful at attracting followers and cash. The Discordians and the Church of Euthanasia also had their adherents. To what degree was the Moorish Orthodox Church just another pot-fueled parody? That depends on who you talked to, and when. As Hakim Bey told me, it was possible and even preferable to embrace *both/and* rather than *either/or*. Is the MOC really less credible than born again clown ministry, saint statues that exude real blood, boy's club Muslim heaven, Tibetan prayer wheels, or weeping televangelists?

Noble Drew Ali had been dead serious, yet he lied about his Egyptian initiation and lifted much of the *Circle Seven Koran* from sources scholars have tracked down and identified. For him, the Moorish Science Temple was not a joke religion, though the turbans, scimitars, fezzes, silk gowns and sashes could easily have come from a B-grade exotica film. The same, however, can be said for the Pope's tiara, writhing blue-skinned shivas, Iroquois false face society masks, and Hassidic fur hats. It's all kitsch. Seen from a slightly skewed angle, all religion is joke religion.

The Church of Latter Days Saints may have started as a teenager's prank, but its millions of adherents certainly don't consider it a joke now. Mormons seldom see their religion as a vast, hugely-popular comedy routine. Their annual Hill Cumorah Pageant (with seven hundred participants on stage) was an endless parade of sleep-inducing sanctimony. *The Book of Mormon* can't be beat as a mother lode of pseudo-ancient tedium. The Prophet Joseph Smith really did get dragged out of jail and lynched. Little of this, in short, sounds like a Laff Riot. If by joke religion you mean an amusing parody or sneering satire, then the Latter Day Saints don't qualify. But Joe Smith was certainly a joker, that is, a clever trickster, a wild card in the stacked deck of American folk religion.

Knowing my fascination with Mormons, especially their origins in folk magic and Freemasonry, Hakim Bey was eager to hear all I could tell him about Joseph Smith the Prophet and his use of rods in divination. At the time Smith was creating the Church of Latter Day Saints, a number of other homespun charlatans criss-crossed America, offering their services as rodsmen who promised to unearth buried Indian gold, Captain Kidd's treasure, stolen and hidden jewels. This frontier treasure-digging economy flourished on my home turf, and reached its pinnacle of absurdity and power in the birth of the Mormon church. Pirate booty became the golden plates of the *Book of Mormon*. The white salamander that guarded the occult treasure was transformed into the Angel Moroni. And rodsmen — who were often only a few steps ahead of the law — rebranded themselves as priests of a new American religion.

The two of us traded back and forth tales of wonder and bald-faced fraud. We both knew there was a proper term for the use of rods in divination, but neither of us could call it to mind, and even his massive unabridged dictionary proved useless in finding the word we wanted.

We both admitted defeat, not easy for two writers who prided themselves on their obscure vocabulary and the depths of their forbidden knowledge. I did though, eventually send him this message:

"The mystery is finally solved. The word we were looking for all those years is RHABDOMANCY (meaning divination using a wand, staff or stick — from the Greek 'rhabdos' — rod). I found it in — of all places — an anti-Catholic screed: Maria Monk's *Awful Disclosures of the Hotel Dieu Nunnery,* which sold 300,000 copies between 1836 and the Civil War."

MOR

At first glance, there's little connection between the Mormons and the Moorish Science Temple, beside the "mor" sound in the names and the American tradition of do-it-yourself religion. One gleams hyper-white, with a long history of racism. The other celebrated the uplift of African people. One keeps growing and is immensely wealthy. The other is down to a few remaining members and not much in the bank.

It's true that the scriptures of both religions were stolen from obscure sources. Both the Prophets Joseph Smith and Noble Drew Ali acquired spurious titles, and were dead soon after leaving jail. Also notable is the absence of inspiring music in both religions. The Mormon Tabernacle Choir (or the Mo-tab to those in the know) produces ponderous sentimental All-American pabulum. Moorish Temple services were, by most accounts, remarkably sedate. There was some chanting, but these were ordinary hymn tunes set to words that reflect the ideals of the Temple. So "Give Me That Old Time Religion" becomes "Moslem's That Old Time Religion." The acronym MOR — in the world of popular radio — stands for Middle of the Road, that is, bland and forgettable. This label applies to both Moorish Science and Mormon music.

Though his appreciation was genuine, and the pleasure he could derive from it quite deep, music was one subject where Hakim Bey's understanding didn't support his pronouncements. He spoke at great length about his love of the boys' choir at Saint Thomas in Manhattan. The music there was indeed wonderful, but his enjoyment had an impressionistic, rather than informed, nature. Smells and bells, gorgeous décor, the procession of winsome young singers in elegant vestments: high church services at Saint Thomas had it all. But for Hakim Bey there was more nostalgia, a longing for a lost and happier world, than actual musical comprehension.

As an infant he was baptized in the Episcopalian church and he insisted that he had a memory of this event. More plausible was his recollection of being confirmed and performing in a church choir until he was eleven or twelve. Nostalgia, loss, yearning all mingled as he told me about those halcyon days. With genuine sadness, he said that if the Anglicans would jettison their morality, sermonizing, sentimentality and bad metaphysics, and keep just the music, the Church might be a welcome place for him, a sanctuary, a real home. Again and again, he sounded this refrain: *Tallis, Byrd, Mundy and the other sixteenth century polyphonists attained a level of mystical rapture to induce a state the equal of any rite in Tantra or Taosim. Seriously, good music IS*

Episcopalian yoga. Anglican Voodoo! What else do you need?

Music was one of the keys to help unlock the mystery for me, or at least pointed me toward certain arcane correspondences. The echo of "mor" in Mormon and Moorish kept ringing in my mind's ear. Then I spoke the acronyms — LDS MOC — as a rhythmic chant. LDS MOC — the letters called forth from deep childhood memory a melody. LDS MOC M-O-U-S-E. It was the theme song from the TV Mickey Mouse club, only lured out of an alternate universe where Annette Funicello was a sexy African prophetess and Uncle Walt sported a black fez.

At the same age as when Hakim Bey sang beautifully in church, I'd chanted this idiotic Disney tune with a dozen others, pounding our feet on the floor of the school bus. The only lines I remember now make reference to holding forever some kind of banner: "High! High! High! High!" I was never a Disney fan. But the endless iteration of the cretinous theme song (which at one point made our bus driver pull over in the middle of a bridge to demand an end to the mad relentless chorus) remains in my mind. New words now sang themselves in my inner ear, and far more powerful letters. "LDS MOC" ringing "High! High! High! High!" like the chant of young cannabis fiends.

Another "More" loomed out of the past. The song with that title, once heard, is not easily forgotten. Starting out as the theme from the sleazy, so-called exotic exploitation film *Mondo Cane* (literally — A Dog's World) it broke big in America in the summer of 1963. Since then, "More" has been covered countless more times with English lyrics. There's no obvious resonance between the low-grade film (also released in the U.S. as *Tales of the Bizarre: Rites, Rituals and Superstitions*) and the haunting melody.

Then came Les Variations, the only French rock band made up of Moroccan Jews to crack America's top 40. Starting out in 1966, they toured Europe covering tunes by Chuck Berry, Little Richard, Elvis, and the Rolling Stones. But by 1975, when I saw them at Rochester's Masonic Temple, Les Variations had mutated into a potent fusion of gritty guitar riffs and North African exotica. Blending into their surging rock clamor traditional Sephardic songs, they were the first band to create Moroccan Roll. Their '74 song of that name still hits my musical G-spot: a Moorish modal riff, loud and loaded stonesy rock, and primitive skirling reed pipe floating in and out of the mix. Their 1975 hit, "Superman, Superman" — while not as interesting as "Moroccan Roll" — brought to the American airwaves a hint of orientalismo.

A last musical "mor" in the chain of connections linked me back to occult headwear. When my collection of fezzes reached seven, I began private vocal lessons. I had no interest in learning to sing prettily. I told my teacher at my first lesson that I wanted to sing louder, faster, and higher. Knowing the traditional American backcountry sound I so loved, she was agreeable.

After a few months of exercises and practice, the first actual song I attempted was the old Irish favorite "Believe Me If All Those Endearing Young Charms." My voice teacher had a Victorian pump organ, perfect accompaniment for this song which pays tribute to the wondrous past and at the same time celebrates the irrelevance of time itself. The word "charm" — originally meaning a musical, magical formula or amulet — caught my attention. I was also drawn to the writer's name: *Thomas* (which means "the twin") and *Moore*.

It was only years later that I discovered the third link between us. Thomas Moore had written the romantic book-length poem, *Lalla Rookh*, after which Rochester's grotto of The Mystic Order of the Veiled Prophets of the Enchanted Realm took its name. By the time I sang Moore's most famous song, I had taken possession of three black fezzes with the name Lalla Rookh stitched on the front in glistening metallic thread.

DEAR TH. (1)

    I've come to feel that sound-recording has been a total catastrophe. Every recording is the tombstone of a piece of living music. (Of course every text is the tombstone of living speech — but with music and recording the effect is more poignant.) Wm. Burroughs said somewhere that "anyone with a frying pan owns death" or words to that effect. Well, everyone with a sound-recording play-back device also owns death. OK — it's a metaphor — but a powerfully visceral metaphor, given that cast-iron frying pans of sound can assault you whenever and wherever the "owner" pleases. (Is your house a refuge of silence? Haw haw — you must be a billionaire!) All the music I hear around me was chosen by someone else, and I have no right (and no way) to refuse it. Isn't this the abyss of literal alienation? Who can I be, in such a situation, other than the other? Even if I choose the music — and inflict it on the others — I'm still nothing more than the consumer of someone else's creativity. I can "choose" anything from pygmy humming to Sun Ra, but the music is never mine. (The ramifications of this are endless, and touch the musician as much as the listener — maybe more so.) Jacques Attalli [sp?] proposed "saving" music through Noise — I would propose that it can only be saved through silence. Everybody, put down the frying pans and listen.

Last night I heard something good. We had a strange storm, thunder rolling thru the long echo'y mountains (Shawangunks) around midnight, a bit of rain pattering on new leaves, a bass-line of bullfrogs glunk-glunking like hicks laughing monotonously at chicken jokes, and a solo by a nightbird that sounds somewhat like a nightingale — I don't know its name. This was a kind of silence — the "silence of Nature" if you like.

Not an argument for anything. Not a "proof" of my theory. "Where every prospect pleases, and only Man is vile"? No — not even that. But — what music!

GRAND METROPOLITAN

Handed over from one Moorish outpost to another, disappearing and reappearing in no discernible pattern, the *Monitor* passed into my hands. Only sixteen pages long, the Preternatural Hygiene issue inaugurated my tenure at the helm.

My first editorial begins *Calling all Moors — past, present, and future! The Moorish Science Monitor has awoken from its brief slumber of rejuvenation and has returned to illuminate, elucidate, execrate and excite!*

I'd produced a modest little zine, and yet I overflowed with excitement. *Like a glorious engine of effulgent joy, it calls to the faithful: open yourselves, make room in your hearts, bowels, minds and souls for the truth that passeth understanding.*

The Ziggurat Lodge of the Moorish Orthodox Church proudly — though with not a little trembling of the innermost viscera — hereby takes on the mantel so nobly worn in the past by Hakim Bey (Moorish Metropolitan of Manhattan), Jacob Rabinowitz (redactor extraordinaire and Evil Step-Mullah of Miss Living Proof) and the mysterious forefathers / mothers / entities in the shadowy and legend-haunted past.

I printed a letter from Hakin Bey, which conferred his blessings on my efforts. *Salaam aliekum! The Manhattan hierarchy of the Moorish Orthodox Church (Adept Chamber) is tickled pink to hear that the Moorish Science Monitor is once again to reach the faithful (and the faithless) this time under your aegis. Not only is your editorship approved, you're also hereby appointed Grand Metropolitan of the Burnt Over District, i.e.: the holy lands of upstate NY. We feel sure that Moorish Orthodoxy will thrive upon such mantic soil.*

In the long tradition of selling implausible magic scrolls, potions and nostrums, together we concocted Fez Brand Moorish Blessing Oil. The label says it all: bright green with a peach-colored fez and ziggurat, and a pair of bright blue hands in brotherly handclasp. *Made by Ziggurat Company Rochester N.Y.* In tiny letters: *For Best Results, Apply Liberally.* What is it? Water with a drop of green food coloring, and (this is crucial) a few flakes of genuine gold foil floating in the murk.

We were inspired by the Moorish health products sold during the Prophet's time. Called by the enemies of the temple — and by some misguided scholars — Voodoo Oils, these were in fact herbal preparations. Moorish Antiseptic Bath Compound was claimed to be beneficial for dandruff, stiff joints, sore feet, and skin troubles when used as a face wash. Also available was Moorish Body Builder and Blood Purifier.

For our blessing oil, Hakim Bey bankrolled the gold foil, so flimsy that static electricity made it almost impossible to work with. He also had the labels printed on fine card stock and trimmed neatly for application to the bottles. One more touch made it twice as authentic. The word "Alleged" is printed below the ziggurat. This is common, almost required, in the catalogs advertising hoodoo cremes, elixirs and nostrums. Black Cat Dejinxing powder, Lucky Planet Oil, Two-head Lotion, Dr. Elijah's Bone-Restoring Panacea, Genuine John the Conqueror Root.

Besides tracts, a set of four sigils, books, and eight-inch tall handmade replicas of Asherah (a Canaanite fertility goddess — "The standard of quality in vulgar superstition"), we sold the Blessing Oil through the *Moorish Science Monitor*. We made almost no money on this operation. The point wasn't to bilk credulous saps into buying scabrous crap. Our intention was far more esoteric. Like hoodoo root doctors, faith healers and the snake-oil salesmen who traveled the back roads of America, we hoped to bring a whiff of the wondrous into otherwise banal lives.

In the nineteenth century, miracle men sold vials of Egyptian darkness. It was all a con of course, just little back bottles corked and sealed up with wax, with nothing inside. But this wasn't merely a scam perpetrated on frontier fools. Like 3 card monte, sawing a lady in half, sleight of hand tricks, and pranks played on religious rubes, a small glass vessel containing nothing but darkness could also serve as an esoteric key. Though supposedly captured in the heart of a pyramid, the darkness was — in literal terms — no different than any other. Yet there was a story that went with these weird vials. Tomb raiders had been looting pyramids for millennia. Except for remarkable finds such as young King Tut, most of the ancient tombs had been scoured clean of precious metals and jewels. What did these depths still contain? Darkness, which like a well kept refilling itself as soon as the looters' torches had disappeared down a dim passageway.

Likewise, Moorish Blessing Oil was a self-renewing resource. There are bottles of it still out there beyond the horizon, working their spurious wonders. There are hundreds of labels still in my possession, and each one is imbued with power, or I should say, each one is alleged to bring a blessing.

CARTOGRAPHIC MYSTERY

Hakim Bey captured the nature of the Burnt Over District (where I've lived my entire life) in an apt two-word phrase: mantic soil. These are, in his words, holy lands. But much more so this place is mantic (which means having the power of divination or prophesy.) And soil? Yes, I inhabit an actual landscape, not a mere political designation with meaningless boundaries.

The Burnt Over District comprises the widest and easiest way through the great Appalachian barrier, which stretches from Labrador all the way to Sand Mountain in Alabama. Since the first landing of white invaders, the Appalachians acted as a gigantic containing wall, holding land-hungry Europeans on the east coast of the continent. In the early 1800s, my region was the prime path to the vastness of the great plains. Here, the Iroquois saw their land as a great longhouse. At one end — my end — were the Seneca, keepers of the western door. On the other side of the state were the Mohawk, keepers of the eastern door. Once the Iroquois were crushed, the great white migration could flood westward. By the time the southern slave-holders' revolt had been put down, the region had become just a place to pass through, a zone where only a faint whiff of spiritual smoke could be detected.

Still, there are a few of us who refuse to forget what happened here. With the appearance of the Public Universal Friend and her followers (the first whites to over-winter in the area) and for about a hundred years after, more spiritual wildness flourished here than any place in the western hemisphere. New religions were born — most notably Mormonism and spiritualism. Shakers, Fourierists, and end-time Jews settled here, though sadly vanished. German Pietists came, expecting the thousand year reign of Jesus, but eventually dissolved into the landscape of normalcy. Apocalyptic manias swept up thousands. It was a time of portents and prophesies. The signs were unmistakable: a cholera epidemic, showers of meteors, rings around the sun and crosses seen in the sky. Halley's comet flashed across the heavens in 1835 and the so-called Great Comet in 1843 was widely interpreted as a portent of the end. The Millerites gathered in joyous expectation of Christ's return.

The ancients stared up at the stars and saw heroes, gods and monsters in the night sky. It's far easier for me to find my mythic emblems on paper, rather than in the far cosmos. So, with a pen and some colored markers, I converted a standard travel map into an esoteric document. Doing magic to maps, Hakim Bey agreed, can change the real landscape. The map is not the territory — *and yet it is*.

First I drew a red circle on the seven major locations that Carl Carmer noted in his book on the Burnt Over District: Lily Dale, Jerusalem, Rochester, Hill Cumorah, Hydesville, Oneida and Watervliet. Then I marked my own more private arcane sites, making dots on the villages where Charles Finney preached in his explosion of revivalist zeal. I've journeyed to all of these villages: Adams (where he had his soul-rending conversion), Antwerp, Gouverneur. He also preached in even smaller hamlets that barely exist now: Evans Mills, DeKalb, Westernville, Theresa. In Rochester he found his Armageddon, the spirit of God possessing him to make his wildest revivalist stand here.

Each daubed with a crimson splotch, these places make a cartographer's constellation, not stars in the sky, but bright spots where the early evangelical fervors burned. If I squint, I can make my hand-drawn pattern laid over New York State resemble an eagle with outstretched wings. But someone else might see a tree with widespread branches, or a dissolving mushroom cloud.

I'm aware that even the most exhaustive map leaves out much that is crucial. Blow up the scale until you see individual houses and barns, ruined churches and washed-out one lane roads, and still the map is incomplete. This makes the maps all the more alluring, each telling a different story.

One which helped me see the true nature of the Burnt Over District was a map that showed the entirety of the canal system that sent out its tentacles in the wake of the Grand Erie's success. Black River Canal north from Rome. Genesee Valley to the Pennsylvania state line. Chenango down to Binghamton. A spur up to Lake Champlain, connecting to Canada. This map is a snapshot of the state's history. Without the Erie feeding in the wealth of the American Midland, New York City would be a fraction of its size. Buffalo, Rochester, and Syracuse would hardly be on the map. All the other canals failed, as railroads took over, leaving behind a few ghost ditches, weird scars and humps in the landscape.

The word "geography" once had allure, fascination, magic. There was a time when maps were not merely simplified pictures of place, but actual keys to opening up the secrets of those places. They were, in short, amulets. And those who possessed these sorcerous charts, and knew how to use them for occult purposes, had true power. They are all, even the most banal, imbued with power. All maps, in short, are treasure maps, even without X-marks-the-spot or a dream of buried gold.

I read a map as I would read a metaphysical mystery story. Murder doesn't interest me, nor do elaborate criminal capers. I have no interest in human cruelty or mere greed, in the violence of stupidity and the stupidity of violence. A map, on the other hand, shows me something far more intriguing than modern savages killing each other or stealing each others' glittering trash. *Where?* Of course that question is made manifest on the map. But also *how* and *when?* And sometimes *why?*

I use the word "metaphysical" in the sense of transcendence, beyond so-called objective reality. Something wondrous strange — a confluence of mysteries — happened in this land. It could be argued that it's just that the miracle of my birth occurred here. It's likely I will die here too and my ashes will be scattered in Mount Hope Cemetery among my ancestors, within sight of the hospital where I was born. This is the place, *my place,* and that's enough to make it mantic. Everyone who lives an entire lifetime in one landscape, and spends countless hours immersed in the past there, might claim the same privileged status for their locale.

I read a map as a fortuneteller reads fate in a palm. Secrets of the past and future lie there, on the crowded page full of tiny names (both banal and weird), colored squiggles, and cryptic symbols. Roads, manmade rivers, railroads (both well used and abandoned): these are the lines in a great geographical palm, to be followed, studied, and interpreted.

Printed on cheap paper, frayed on the edges and weakened at the seams, made to be consulted and then discarded, tourism maps are the perfect form of ephemera. Like the seven-inch 45 rpm single, or twenty-five cent paperbacks, these maps were made to be used a few times and then tossed out. Those that survive, especially those well-worn, acquire a certain value — though seldom in a monetary sense.

Decades ago I began marking on an ordinary road map all the routes I've taken through New York State. Highlighted in brilliant yellow, my paths create a steadily expanding web, like the underground threads that make forests into a vast hidden fungal network. With the passage of time, more and more of the glowing threads appear, a golden web superimposed on the state.

First I filled in the main routes, the standard paths to places I've been a hundred times. Over the years though, I've taken increasingly obscure roads, choosing to travel in a seemingly random manner, losing myself and finding myself again on the map. Driving with little idea where I was, I often discovered hidden delights. A full-scale concrete brontosaurus in a farmer's front yard. A Tyrolean restaurant which seemed to have been abandoned in a hurry. The Seneca Torture Tree and its commemorative wayside shrine.

I've kept the map for decades, opening it carefully each time to add my inch or two of newly-broken golden terrain. Connect the dots, fill in this little loop of light gray (a local road) or that thicker red line (a county highway), this famous cult site, that totally obscure place where an act of American sorcery had occurred. The map is a way of organizing memory. Yes, I've been there, and there, and *there*. I count it as evidence, testimony below the level of reason.

The places are mine if I've passed through them. The details, the actual textures of the places, are more real if I've recorded my fleeting presence there.

One particularly dense and luminous web is in the Hudson Valley / Catskill region, marking all the trips I've taken, exploring the misty past and imaginal future with Hakim Bey.

THE GRANGE

In our letters back and forth we recounted adventures in psycho-geographical wandering. I told him about visiting the Ephrata Cloister, searching for the Taughannock Giant in Trumansburg, exploring the Grotto of the Agony, getting a peak at the Tiffany windows in Albion, and talking my way into the Church of the Hypercube.

After a trip to Centre Hall, I wrote to tell him of a tour I took at the Progress Grange, helping a friend scout locations for a Sacred Harp singing event. The lower floor was standard late 1890s social space. But upstairs things got a lot stranger, tricked out with all sorts of Grange ritual impedimenta. My favorite was the carved wooden owl beneath which the gatekeeper held his post. It was disorienting, these rural salt of the earth types talking about being the Ceres and Flora and Pomona, needing certain people in certain places to esoterically open the lodge, and having no idea what the ritual or mythic meanings were for their ceremonial roles.

I enclosed the flyer our guide gave us, describing the annual Grange encampment: over 900 tent sites, used every year (and highly prized) since 1890. Most of the flyer was standard county fair trivia (will we ever escape the plague of Elvis imitators?) The campgrounds were right in the middle of Centre Hall, and it looked like a cross between a concentration camp (barbed wire all around, windowless buildings) and an abandoned grass parking lot. The event draws big crowds of backcountry folks, but how much of the original Grange attitude remains was unclear. Our guide bragged at length about Worthy Master Rhone and how he was instrumental in getting antitrust laws passed and Rural Free Delivery mail instituted. And the whole time the smell of that night's roast beef dinner was wafting upwards.

Hakim Bey wrote back:

Kelpius influenced the founders of Ephrata. Last I heard, there were still "five old ladies" in Virginia, the last Sabbatarian Baptists (the official name of the Ephrata sect) — like the last five Shakers of Sabbath Day Lake, who seem to have attained immortality. And what about the Schwenckfeldians? — the only organized remnant of the "Spiritual Church" movement to reach Pennsylvania — do they persist? Should we join them? Or what about the New Church (Swedenborgians)? (Just fantasizing, really. These fossilized esotericisms are nice, but . . .) I'm reading Swedenborg's Dream Book, also skimming a weird 19th C. American tract giving a Swedenborgian interpretation of Fourier. Where do I sign up?

Then he told about attending the meeting of the Accord Patroon Grange. *I went with my neighbor Chris who'd agreed to address them on bee keeping. I think I pointed out the Hall to you once. Very strange, rather moving experience. Physically: the Jukes, bordering on Lovecraft. (I'm not exaggerating.) Décor: 1952. Age: from zero to 100, mostly the latter. Mood: sweet as pumpkin pie. Sentiments: vaguely Populist, even a bit anti-Capitalist. Salute of Flag. Christian hymns. Hot dogs and cake. Chris and I drove back along Towpath Rd. in starry dark (his family used to own the whole area), stopped to smoke a joint at the swimming hole, talked about joining the Grange . . . more fantasy. But I'll keep on sending them money from time to time.*

I'm hoping for a long snowy winter — just realized I'm working on 4 books at once (incl. the NY Hist. essays, which I meant to finish last year). But — before the snows — do you want to go look for the Ramapo Salamander?

COMICS

A spot next to the table where Hakim Bey worked was the home of his fat, one-volume encyclopedia. The spine was split and unraveling, the pages tattered and food-stained. Around it were drifts of dog-eared catalogs, magazines, flyers for events long past, and zines from far and near. But, because he often consulted it for facts that did not come immediately to mind, the encyclopedia was never buried. We'd be discussing any of a hundred arcane subjects and would be momentarily stumped. What was the name of Napoleon's horse? (Marengo.) What was Vivaldi's nickname? (The Red Priest.) What was the correct spelling of the capital of Mongolia? (Ulan Bator.)

He'd say we needed to consult *The Junior Woodchucks' Guidebook and Reservoir of Inexhaustible Know-ledge*, and heft the great volume onto the table, propping it on a pile of papers and dirty dishes. He called it by this cartoon name because of his love for Donald Duck comic books. Without apology, he announced, *Always been a duck man myself.* Huey, Dewey, and Louie were Donald's nephews, and were members of the Junior Woodchucks, an imaginary fraternal organization that had a place of honor in Hakim Bey's inner world. In Carl Barks' Donald Duck comics, the *Guidebook* contained information on every possible subject. The massive volume which Hakim Bey consulted was not quite so exhaustive, but we often found the facts we needed to continue our esoteric palavering.

His obsessions came and went, but there remained a deep vein of love for Amercian pop culture, especially those elements beneath serious consideration (and which he'd enjoyed as a boy.) Krazy Kat, Popeye, and Little Lulu were deathless works of art. His interest in Tintin, Donald Duck, and Little Nemo in Slumberland (which he deemed a masterpiece of visionary art) never had the flavor of stultifying study. They may have been preserved and over-analyzed by academic hacks, but for Hakim Bey, they were well-springs of delight and inspiration.

He wrote to tell me about his latest obsession: "Our Boarding House" with Major Hoople, by Gene Ahern. He'd just ordered $50 worth of photocopies from the Cartoon Library at Ohio State University, and was planning a tribute of some sort to this great American character and fez-wearer, on whose personality he had to some extent modeled himself and his writing style.

As was often the case, Hakim Bey would make an offhand reference and I would then go hunting to see what I could find at the end of the misty trail. I was granted another glimmer of understanding when he told me that a largely-forgotten cartoon character was an inspiration for his life and his written work. In public forums, on the radio and interviewed on camera, he presented himself as a serious — though not humorless or sanctimonious — explorer of esoteric thought. The writer behind all those books, the prophet of the TAZ, the relentless critic of technopathocracy, seldom allowed others to see the smiling wizard behind the curtain. But he'd said it with no hedging or hesitation: Major Hoople was his role model.

The creator-cartoonist explained that Major Amos Hoople had been based on a Civil War veteran who told tall tales and puffed himself as a general, when in fact he'd reached no higher rank than sergeant, and whose boasts of soldierly heroism were all invented to impress anyone whose ear he could bend. Some have compared the major to W. C. Fields, but Falstaff is a better match: obese, blustering, full of himself and a hundred improbable tales, a buffoon whose pathos sometimes showed through his blowhard bragging.

My first encounter with Major Hoople was in a collection of Tijuana Bibles that Hakim Bey allowed me to peruse one night. Like zines, these eight page sex comics barely show up on literary radar. Sold under the counter from the '30 through the '60s, they were pornography of a lost world. In some the art was wretched and shoddy, in other it was exquisite, even if filthy. Clearly, some well-known cartoon artists made some extra money putting pop culture figures through obscene adventures. Popeye, Dick Tracy,

Dagwood, and Li'l Abner all made appearances in these rated-X booklets. Donald Duck does Daisy. Movie stars, Tarzan, Betty Boop, Hitler, Gandhi, and Aunt Jemima also get their kicks. Major Hoople makes an appearance too, his absurd tale-telling goosed up with naked native maidens on a far off island, comically huge erections, flying sweat-drops, and the major's hyperbolic narrative touches. "To that primitive girl goes the credit of giving me the greatest hard-on of my long career." Learning that he must return to civilization, he and the "most sensuous dancer of her race" have sex continually day and night. "I've since learned that at periods of nine months, she has given birth to twins, triplets, and quadruplets — all mine!"

THE GIFTS OF THE FEZZI

I traveled two hundred miles, just beyond the nebulous boundary of the Burnt Over District, packin' black fez. That is, I drove due east to a little village near Albany, to sing nineteenth century American hymns from the *Sacred Harp,* and secretly transfer one item of pseudo-Moroccan headgear. In the trunk of my car was a black tarboosh: my gift for a strange child I would never meet.

About a hundred people had gathered in Voorheesville, none of them (as far as I knew) on a similar mission. We did eighty-three loud hymns in one day (including "Tribulation," "The Last Words of Copernicus," "Babylon is Fallen," "The Grieved Soul," and "The Dying Friend") and ate far too much potluck food. During lunch, I went out to my car to get the fez in question: black felt, too small for my massive cranium, with the Mokanna-head emblem on the front.

The transfer was made over heaped plates of pulled pork, dilly beans, and homemade ice cream. I passed my precious cargo to a charming, remarkably short woman who had told me a few months before (also in a room full of loud obsessional old song singers) that her grandson (grandly named Dash) would love to own a fez.

I never got to meet the boy and expected no communication with him. The anonymity of the gift added to the mystique of the moment. Later, I imagined, somewhere east of the Hudson River, Dash was cheerfully sporting a black Grotto Prophet fez. I never found out what happened inside his prepubescent skull while wearing the arcane Mediterranean headgear. Would he achieve an exalted state (prophesy? orientalismo dreams? singing ancient songs?) Or would the fez get tossed in the closet and be rediscovered years later — a forgotten artifact of childhood?

To maintain the balance (there is no such thing as coincidence in such cases) another fez appeared at my house a few months later. A good friend of Dash's grandmother — she too was a devoted singer of the old American hymns preserved in the *Sacred Harp* — had heard about our clandestine exchange and brought me a genuine fez from Egypt. Inside is a handwritten note: "Fez — purchased in Cairo in May 1960 by George Loft."

The lining appears to be made of fine woven reeds, with stitching that travels around the interior like the path of a planet through the night sky. The label is mostly in Arabic script, though the name El-Hag Ahmed Serag and Son, and the street address of their shop, is printed at the center. Most curious is the circle of printed paper that serves as the underside of fez's flat top. It seems to be an imitation of crocodile skin, though the scales are pinkish-red instead of Nilotic slime green.

Traditional maroon, with no emblems on the outside, after a half century the fez is still in perfect condition, and has pride of place behind me as I write these words.

SNAKES AND LADDERS

When next I visited, Hakim Bey happily showed off a Snakes and Ladders game a friend had found for him in a resale shop. He was thrilled to have it in his possession, remembering it fondly from his childhood and seeing it as yet another irruption of the marvelous into everyday life. I'd played the game too as a kid, though mine was of a newer vintage and was called Chutes and Ladders.

It originated in India as Moksha Patam — the Path of Salvation — and was brought to England in the 1890s. It's a game of pure luck — or pure fate — without a bit of skill involved. You throw the die and move your token. In some versions the snakes represent vices. If you hit one of those squares, you slide down to a lower level. Ladders stand for virtues — giving you a quick trip upward on the board. It's a game that little kids can play. No reading is necessary, just the six pips on the die. But it's also a tool for esoteric contemplation, a map of the karmic universe.

In India, Hakim Bey had encountered the worship of nagas, a race of semi-divine beings that can take shape as half human and half snake, or wholly serpentine. They're usually associated with bodies of water, from wells to seas, and are often guardians of treasure. I pointed out that this sounded like Mormon mythology: Joseph Smith meeting a snake creature that becomes an angel, and who guards the golden plates on which *The Book of Mormon* were written. This aetheric doubling came as no surprise, as these snake-beings are almost universal: Mesopotamia, Buddhism, Hinduism, the Rainbow Snake of Australian aborigines, Mama Wata in the African diaspora, the white trash snake handlers in Alabama.

This led us to talking about Bram Stoker's *Lair of the White Worm*, which he declared to be absolutely the worst novel ever written by a writer of note. I'd read *Dracula* and *The Jewel of the Seven Stars* (Stoker's egyptomania novel), but until then avoided the White Worm. I wasn't surprised that Hakim Bey's assessment was again dead right. The novel is rabidly racist (the African "voodoo man" is described as being "devilridden," "savage," "hideous," "the lowest and most loathsome of all created things which were in some form ostensibly human.") The prose is cloddishly clumsy, the plot is incoherent (including a giant kite to scare off an inexplicable bird invasion), and the concluding pay-off for the reader is nonexistent. Even H.P. Lovecraft, the patron saint of turgid, plotless story-telling, wrote that Stoker "utterly ruins a magnificent idea by a development almost infantile."

The 1988 movie was not quite so dismal. Ken Russell plays up the kitsch elements, the Worm and its sexy avatar are entertaining, and the director does include one stylish touch: a Scottish bagpiper calling the great albino serpent from its hole.

What I found charming about *The Lair of the White Worm* was its linkage between myth and landscape. Supposedly based on the legend of the Lambton worm, Stoker's story might have been a worthy addition to the lore of reptilian spirits of place. Though the tale took many forms, it was based on an actual place, the Lambton Estate near the Scots border. Some claimed that "Jabberwocky" is based on the legend and perhaps there is also a connection to the Loch Ness monster.

Then we wandered down another winding pathway. Hakim Bey mentioned again that we still needed to find the Ramapo Salamander. It would be a bit of a drive, but next time I came down, we could search it out.

DEAR TH. (2)

Now that I know you're saving our letters, I'll try to do better. For a start, I enclose a "tract," first draft, for your comments and corrections. This was eleven pages long, handwritten, and was called "Jesus the Failure." Some of it ended up in the *Black Fez Manifesto*. Some of it remains in my stack of our correspondence, unpublished.

In the thirty-seven years I knew Hakim Bey, we had our two-man conclaves, we talked for hours on the phone, and he even suggested, regarding a possible visit, that we should consult telepathically. But it was the written word — books, articles, letters — that served as our real lifeline. He made it plain how much he valued our epistolary tentacles tangling on the astral plane. *I do appreciate your letters — perhaps the last literate letters that will ever be written to be posted in envelopes — all saved in my Archive for your future biographers.*

Though he lived in a vast hoard of papers that others someday may sort through, I doubt that all my mail remains. At one point he had a secret vault built inside the collapsing harness shop next to his place on the Wallkill. There he stored an unknown number of boxes, filled with his manuscripts, photos, maps, and correspondence. The vault was well constructed, tight and secure, but it was made of wood. Eventually the building that surrounded the archive collapsed. Vines choked the ruin. The rain and snow came — the vault and its contents dissolved into the earth.

I'm not a hoarder, but I preserved all of our correspondence — including the ephemera he passed along. He was very clear that he wanted me to save all the mail that connected us, calling me his last literary correspondent. As my letter writing friends capitulated and shifted over to the technology that had earlier killed the zines, at last only Hakim Bey remained.

Looking forward to seeing me, and heading together into the partially-reenchanted landscape, he wrote, *The season once again approaches for . . . amateur history escapades . . . Current priorities: 1) locate Pang Yang ruins and graveyard (disciples of Universal Public Friend, degenerated into "Jukes") very near. 2) High Tor — scene of Rosicrucian legend of Salamander — long drive down to Haverstraw — possible nearby Indian sites could be added for full day excursion.*

In another letter, he responded to my report on visiting the Oneida perfectionist community by recounting an adventure he'd had with another car-owning friend.

One odd thing about your (ad)ventures into the "19th century" — which I quite envy — & by the way, why wouldn't you want to live there full-time if you *could, knowing what you know now? — one odd thing, I say, is that you needed to use a car to get to them. I'd spend more time in the 19th century if I had a car (or better yet a chauffeur).*

Interruption:

Next day: I've been to the Hardenburgh Mts out in W. Ulster Co. — gorgeous & nearly empty of (ugh) humanity on a late-ripe misty summer day. And why? Because the Rockefellers own the whole damn area except for what the state keeps vacant (for watershed I'd guess) & two monasteries, one Xtian and one Zen, that are grandfathered in — & one little country store, whose owner refused to sell to the R's, as she proudly told us. We visited a state park with a ruined (& I'd say haunted) manor house of Sam Coykendall, a wellknown 19th c. railway king — & a lake mirroring misty mountains. Very few people. On our way to Hardenburgh it occurred to us that "von Hardenberg" was the real name of the poet Novalis. Somewhere along the route we saw a public library book sale — where we found an anthology of Romantic Lit — with a few bits of Novalis, 25 cents — which we took to a very romantic meadow with sacred-shaped mountain view — & read a beautiful quote about Nature as living, & the intuitive philosopher, "wild and without laws," who treats nature as a living being, as opposed to the man of reason who experiences it as dead — indeed kills it.

MEET THE MOORS

One of the favorite features of the *Monitors* I edited was "Meet the Moors." For this, I took pictures of various people sporting a fez from my collection. Some were dedicated members of the MOC with serious intent and deep Moorish knowledge. Some floated in and out, drawn by Hakim Bey's shadowy anarcho glamour. Some were just friends who I'd inveigled into sitting for a few pictures, little knowing that they'd end up with a fake Moorish name and imaginal description in the *Monitor*.

I appear as Ammahl "the Noisome One," twin of Ahmed, "the Human Cooling Tower." I have fangs and he's got bulging eyes. There is Yusef Yusef and Omar Double X — "the Sexecutioner." Rabbi Jon 9 appears, making a hypnotic gesture á la Mandrake the Magician. Ustaz Ta'ammi 3X is declared "Mr. Mental Hygiene 1943." There was also a spread featuring Haqq Shahid ("The Thought Monger"), Strix Nebulosa, Dawud Iblis, and Ix Nur Ix ("The Distresser.") Absurd, ridiculous, juvenile? Yes. But as one of the earliest Shriners (whose fezzes make up most of my collection) explained in the late 19th century: "Little boys dress up and play cowboys and Indians. Men grow up and play at being Arabs." Though I took a picture of Hakim Bey in his best fez, with a wry smile and a forefinger to his temple, as though thinking up a new scheme, to my knowledge no image of him ever appeared in the *Monitor*.

In the Autumn 1994 issue, Sir Richard Burton — "Moorish Saint and Hero" — gets a two page spread, devilishly handsome and wearing a natty fez. Burton was, like many other wild-eyed Europeans of his time, much taken with Islam. As an agent in the Great Game of Empire, he saw himself superior to Indians and Africans. Among Arabs, however, he felt he was among equals. To the British, he was a brilliant, perverse, good-for-nothing rakehell. The Arabs saw his greatness, as a translator, soldier, scholar, explorer, linguist, and teller of tales.

One of his most remarkable feats was penetrating Mecca, not merely sneaking in as a spy (when being found out would have meant death), but performing the entire pilgrimage as a hadji. Was he a true Muslim? The haj, the fact that he memorized huge portions of the Quran, passing for a Sufi among Sufis, treated by Mullahs with the respect due to men of their position: all of this is strong evidence. But of course "true Muslim" is a meaningless term, just as useless as "authentic Christian" or "genuine Jew." For a man of Burton's magnitude, it was important, but not the sole defining element. His life included enough experience for a dozen men. One of the explorers who searched for the source of the Nile, translator of *The Thousand and One Nights and a Night*, joining up with the Ismailis (the so-called

Assassins), crossing America to Salt Lake City in order to mingle with the Mormons, posing as a snake-worshipping Hindu holy man: none of these are in conflict with his love of Islam.

It was story — in the very best and highest sense of that word, neither true nor false, but full of power. Before he began his translation of the *Nights*, he collected manuscripts and oral versions, and traveling the Moslem world, would entertain the lofty and the lowly, sheiks and camel-drivers, with his recitations. For him, the words were what mattered. He wrote over fifty major works and is thought to have mastered at least two dozen languages of five continents. So then — true believer or master of the story? Literal Muslim or great man self-created out of language? It was obvious to me into which category Burton fell.

STAY IRRATIONAL

When next we met in plenary session — that is, eating at our favorite Lebanese restaurant — a stranger with secrets revealed himself.

As we dug into our baba ganoush and dolmades, and Hakim Bey explained that for decades the fez could only be made in the city of Fez, in Morocco, an old man sidled over and said, "I wasn't eavesdropping, but I couldn't help overhearing your conversation. If you want to see three cultures, three centuries, in one bus ride, you must go from Rabat to Marrakesh to Fez." In any social situation, it seemed that Hakim Bey knew everyone of interest, yet this wizened specter was a stranger.

I asked if he'd been to Morocco and he gave a solemn nod. "A beautiful country." Then he explained (or tried to explain) how traveling the roads from one Moroccan city to another was like traveling in time. I asked him if he had a genuine fez from Fez, but he either didn't hear me or didn't want to say.

He returned to his "layers of time" and the amazing bus trip he'd taken. I couldn't tell if this journey had been the year before or half a century ago. A tourist or a spiritual seeker? This wasn't clear either.

"You must go to Fez. It's timeless, deeper than medieval." For a few more moments, Hakim Bey was not the center of attention. The old man spieled on about the market where they sell sparrows in little bamboo cages, the savor of incense mingling with freshly cut cedar wood, the plaintive cries of beggars competing with bleating sheep, horse bells and the hammering of metal workers. He leaned in closer and whispered that we must go to the spell shops of Fez, where we could buy chameleon legs and owl talons to ward off evil desert spirits.

Then he said, with a sigh and a smile, "Have you read Paul Bowles? A wonderful writer. He lived for fifty years in Morocco."

Hipsters and existentialists embraced Bowles' most famous book, *The Sheltering Sky*. Dissolute expats flee into the Sahara — drugs and disgusting insects — aimless wandering and pointless infidelity. The end of the book is a dismal spin on *The Sheik*: an American girl becomes the sexual property of a North African brute. Unlike the story that made Valentino famous, however, there's no romance, just irrational suicidal impulses and ego death in the face of the Sahara's vast bleakness.

When I got home, I went digging into the boxes of old books stashed in the crawl space of my attic. Deep in darkness, I found a seventy-year-old copy of *The Sheltering Sky*. The cover is typical of sleazy paperbacks from the '50s. Published by Signet (which had made millions on Mickey Spillane and James Bond novels) my copy of Bowles' book has a lurid cover painting that shows a vaguely Arabic-looking woman with barely concealed breasts. She lies back lasciviously, looking toward a candle flame, as though it is the flickering heart of passion. An American man, clearly lusting for this Moroccan beauty, holds her hand and gazes on her. The blurb at the top reads, "Strange Romance in the Exotic Desert."

Strange indeed. The scene depicted on the cover is in the text, though totally devoid of romance. The main character has followed a Moroccan man, a primitive pimp, into a hidden encampment. A young girl is brought into the tent. What follows is a confused collision of lust and colonial commerce, from which the American flees as from a nightmare of failed crime.

Stay irrational. Hakim Bey could spin out yarns that lasted all day. But he could also capture the truth in a two word phrase. After reading my next letter, in which I described my cheap paperback copy of *The Sheltering Sky*, he exhorted me to hold onto my dream-life and obsessions. He usually ended his letters with *Wa Salaam* (which means "peace.") He signed off this time with a different closing. I used a xerox machine to blow up the bottom corner of the letter, framed his exhortation, and hung it over my bed. *Stay irrational.*

DR. OMAR

Hollywood, in its heyday, was prone to charmingly weird cultural make-believe. Charlie Chan — the highly esteemed Chinese detective — was portrayed by three different white men. Mr. Moto, his Japanese counterpart, was played by Peter Lorre, a German. For *The Good Earth*, a major studio effort about Chinese peasantry, both leads went to actors who were born in eastern Europe. Boris Karloff — an Englishman with a fake Russian name — portrayed the insidious Dr. Fu Manchu. His insidious daughter — Myrna Loy — was earlier menaced and romanced by the fake Arab, Ramon Novarro (who was Mexican.) Rudolph Valentino — half Italian and half French — played the sexy Bedouin chieftain in *The Sheik*. However, Victor Mature was the greatest cinematic jack-of-all-ethnic-trades.

The most noteworthy Hollywood actor to sport a fez is probably Sydney Greenstreet in *Casablanca*. After that comes Boris Karloff as Ardeth Bey, in *The Mummy*. A distant third is Stepin Fetchit shambling around a pyramid tomb, mumbling incomprehensible drivel — or arcane secrets — in *Charlie Chan in Egypt*. These roles are much deserving of my admiration. But it's Victor Mature, as the mysterious

Dr. Omar, who has the strongest claim to true Moorish sainthood.

He started out on Broadway, in a dream sequence from the pseudo-Freudian show *Lady in the Dark*, playing a silent circus strongman. His career boomed, and just before the U.S. entered World War Two, he starred in *The Shanghai Gesture*. Though movie-land's greatest emblem of racial confusion — playing Hannibal, Crazy Horse, Samson, an Ottoman Turk, an Egyptian, Zarak Khan (an Afghan chief), a Christian Jew, an Irish huckster, a caveman, and a sixty foot grinning giant (see: *Head*) — he is not in this case a fake Chinese. As Dr. Omar, he first appears in the back of an open car, edging slowly through the crowded streets of Shanghai. He wears a broad, lustrous cape, or burnoose, and a fez. The first words he speaks on screen are: "Allah be praised."

Later we find out that he's half-Armenian, and a mix of other nationalities, born somewhere in the middle east. But his ethnicity is never well-defined. He praises Allah one more time, and makes a hand gesture that's reminiscent of a Catholic crossing himself, but it's supposed to be somehow a marker of his vague (never mentioned) Muslim background.

He's a crypto-pimp, picking up a sexy blond American chorus girl (saving her from arrest by paying off the police) and bringing her to Madame Gin Sling's casino, where numerous women seem to be for sale, or rent. (In the play the film is based on, the procuress is named Mother God Damn, but Hollywood couldn't handle such irreverence in 1942.) The madam is a fake Chinese: Ona Munson with hideous lacquered curls of hair and an arachnid smile. We never see Dr. Omar sell the sexual favors of any woman, but his business, as "middleman," certainly is shady.

He smokes a lot of cigarettes, demonstrates no medical skill, pouts his preternaturally-lush lips, and lounges about in a fez doing nothing in particular. Yet in the poster for the film, we see him about to kiss the gorgeous "Eurasian" Gene Tierney. His fez is ox blood red and Gene's face is flushed pink, appearing to be overcome with erotic feelings. The tag line: "Shanghai — where almost anything can happen ... and does!"

Most of the film was shot on one large set: the casino, which is always packed with gamblers, whores, gawkers, slummers, and Eric Blore as a cripple on a crutch. It has a claustrophobic feel. No one will ever escape, once the gravitational pull of the spinning roulette wheel has grabbed them.

What exactly is the Shanghai Gesture? We never find out. Walter Huston, the evil English capitalist who comes to destroy Madame Gin Sling, is described as making a compulsive up-thrust of his arm in times of heightened emotion. Only once do we see him do this. It looks like a fascist salute, but politics are never mentioned in the film. Perhaps the explanation was lost on the cutting room floor.

Or perhaps it's a symbol that the director — Josef von Sternberg — wanted to leave as an unsolved mystery.

As I write these words, I have a framed picture of Victor Mature looking over my shoulder. As Dr. Omar, he holds in his right hand a fob or mystic doo-dad. Under his cloak are evening clothes. And those lips — lush, pouty, cruel, feminine — are unnerving on a guy six feet three and muscled like a side show strongman. His fez is canted so that we get a glimpse of his gleaming brilliantined hair. The tassel on his fez dangles fetchingly to the side, a perfect touch of Hollywood orientalismo.

"THE DOG" AND ISLAM

Preparing the God/Dog issue of the *Monitor*, I asked Hakim Bey for his thoughts on the subject. I received in reply the following, which he instructed me to print as a letter to the editor.

"The Dog" and Islam

The dog is the "carnal self" and thus while the ordinary Moslem despises the dog, the sufi can tame it thru love. I've always thought that dogs are solar while cats are lunar, and that Islam as a lunar religion, favors the cat. The only exception to the rule against dogs in the house or tent or against sharing food from the same plate as a dog (which is okay with cats) is the Saluki, or Egyptian/Persian lionhound. Most courageous of all paleolithic hunting dogs, the Saluki does not bark, tracks by sight not smell, and can outrun a cheetah. Altho the Saluki (like its prey) is pure solar, it also seems to be sort of an honorary cat and thus "clean." The Prophet said, "Cats are clean and keep watch round about us," ie: for malevolent psychic entities. Thus the cat is "psychic" while the dog is "sarkic" (flesh versus the soul). Moslems call Christians "dogs" because Jesus is solar, being associated with dogs. Jesus is holy but unclean, because he overthrew the law of cleanliness, the Mosaic dispensation which Islam in a sense reestablishes (and which Sufism in turn deconstructs). An Irish friend of mine, a scholar of Persian, once called the English a nation of dog-worshippers; and esoterically he was right. Christ crucified is a dog, God spelled backwards, God dispelled, the spell broken by reversal, God in defeat — an image of horror to the average Moslem. Christianity and Sufism however sympathize with the Deus Patheticus, the God incomplete without his lovers, as the dog is incomplete without its master.

SORCERERS

Renting a boat, Hakim Bey and a friend went to Esopus Island for the day. They wanted to see if they could find a trace of Aleister Crowley, who had established a camp there decades before. Soon after their return, I'd gotten a call and a report on this day-trip into the imaginal realms.

Aleister Crowley — the so-called wickedest man in the world — had indeed traveled up the Hudson River from New York City to Esopus Island. But that had been during World War One. Traces? Was there anything left? Legend had it that he'd painted sigils and symbols on the cliff sides, so that people going up the river would be confronted by esoteric truths. "Let 'Do What Thou Wilt' Be the Whole of the Law" was Crowley's most famous saying. Supposedly, river travelers would have experienced uncanny impulses and troubling dreams after passing Crowley's island haunt.

Though there were no great revelations, Hakim Bey's pleasant little voyage had been worth the time, effort, and expense. He didn't find much, but he claimed that he had a good idea where the sigils would've been. As was often the case, he had to imagine the evidence on his sojourns. Extraordinary events had happened there. But nature, and the ravages of civilization, had effaced any signs. He and I had to project what we knew (the story) onto what we saw (the ordinary places.)

Over the years, the name Aleister Crowley had come up in our conversations. Back in the '70s, Jimmy Page, of Led Zeppelin fame, had owned Equinox, an occult bookshop in London. The store didn't last long, but Hakim Bey had gone there and admired the great collection of esoteric doodads and mystic tomes, especially the Crowleyite arcana. Jimmy hadn't been around, and if he had been, I doubt Hakim Bey would've been impressed. It was Crowley who interested him, not the multimillionaire rock star who dabbled in pop-cult Satanism.

An earlier point of contact for me was through one of Crowley's books of turgid poetry. A friend in college had been propositioned by one of his professors in an oblique manner, the professor giving him a copy of *White Stains* and asking what he thought of it. My friend was both puzzled and disgusted by the poems and passed the book on to me for my opinion. Called by one of Crowley's most admiring biographers, "exceedingly filthy," its homoerotic content is less clear than Crowley's nauseous imagination. The professor wisely used the college's copy of the bait, not his own. He made no overt overtures, though years later my friend said that if he'd given a more positive response, he might've traveled the world as the professor's young gunsel. A while after graduation, I went back to the college library, to search out

White Stains (wondering what names I would find written on the borrower's card.) The book, and all of Crowley's poetry, had vanished from the collection.

Visiting Hakim Bey, whose place was always crowded with tottering stacks of books, I found Colin Wilson's *The Occult.* Gingerly easing it out of a four-foot high tower, I thumbed through and found the chapter called "The Beast Himself." Wilson is said by some to have written too many books, too quickly. This one however, first published in 1971, is packed with fascinating ideas. His treatment of Crowley is neither hysterically negative nor fawning — the usual responses. He gives Crowley three dozen pages, focusing largely on the will, with which — he claims — Crowley was enormously endowed. Why did he need magic, Wilson asks, if the amazing effects are the product of human will? The answer is at the heart of this nearly 800-page book. The will can not operate in a vacuum. "It needs a whole scaffolding of drama, of conviction, of purpose." In short, it needs showmanship

Wilson never fully defines the deep instinctive will that he claims is crucial to occult power. If he is right, though, what matters most is the force of attention and intention. But it needs a stage, a story, props and utterances, symbolic action — in other words, theater — to fully manifest. Wilson's will is not mere desire: I want this, I covet that, I'm drawn, pulled, enslaved by attraction. He returns repeatedly to this central idea: "Occultism is not an attempt to draw aside the veil of the unknown, but simply the veil of banality that we call the present." We live, most of us most of the time, in a trance. We forget, or ignore, the immense world of broader significance that stretches around us.

Sorcery is, according to Hakim Bey, a will-driven system of enhanced consciousness and the deployment of this non-ordinary awareness to bring about desired results in the apparent world. Or, as he said more than once, in far simpler terms: *I demand marvelous secrets!*

It seems a contradiction, but men of imaginative will (such as Crowley at the height of his powers) are intensely engaged in the real texture of the world. "Our normal more-or-less-bored state of everyday consciousness arises from the habit of devaluing the world. Instead of saying 'How fascinating,' we yawn." Then we shuffle on to the next meaningless task or distraction. The opposite of this is magic.

I borrowed *The Occult* and started at the beginning, finished Wilson's book and never returned it. With a nearly luminous alien-green cover, and with the subtitle "The Ultimate Book for Those Who Would Walk with the Gods," it remains to this day on my shelves, side by side with *The Great Beast*, an early biography of Crowley, which reached a wide audience, from Jimmy Page to teenaged nobodies who were also caught in the occult web. Wanting to go to the sources, I ordered a copy long after it had been made irrelevant by other, much better, biographies.

My well-worn copy came in the mail, from the other side of the country. Inside was a pink sticky-note with this message: "Greetings from the upper left temple." Below that was a number 7 inside a circle. "Upper left" on the map is Oregon or Washington, but to this day I have no idea which Moorish Orthodox adept had taken my order and packaged the book for mailing.

The Great Beast is full of magical gibberish, spells that Crowley supposedly used. Far more important to me was the photo that takes up most of the back cover. Once seen, the image is not soon — if ever — forgotten. Crowley stares directly at the viewer with a fierce gaze. It's not evil, but confidence and concentration that I see there, as though he were still alive and looking at me, through me. The placement of the hands adds to the effect of the photo. He presses them to the sides of his face (palms back, thumbs cocked) not so much squeezing his face as framing it and focusing the psychic power he claimed to possess. He wears a black hat that on another man would look absurd, a soft triangle that works a visual rhythm with his hieratic hand gesture. On the front of the hat is the eye of Horus in a smaller triangle. This has been called his Third Eye, or the All-Seeing Eye on top of the Freemasonic pyramid. He doesn't look malign in the picture, or dissolute. It's power that comes through. I felt it the first time my eyes met his and I imitated the hand placement to stare back at him.

Heroin addict — cokehead — sexual predator — prodigal rich boy, then leech — at best a writer of mediocre ability (though deluded that he was in the same class as Shakespeare) — egomaniac supreme: Aleister Crowley was all of these. Any one of them describes an odious bore. Combined, they should make him ten times more repulsive and wretched. Yet he caught my eye (the photo), my interest (the satanic reputation), and my ambivalent admiration.

It wasn't Crowley's so-called wickedness that intrigued me. It was his shadowy mixture of success and failure, self-promotion and secrecy. He failed again and again. Though a brilliant mountaineer, he failed in his attempt on Kangchenjunga (third highest peak in the world.) His books reached only a small audience in his lifetime. His new religion had very few adherents, most of them mentally ill or alcoholic. He was chased out of his Abbey of Thelema and it stood abandoned for years. His claim to absurd aristocratic titles and his petty feuds with other occult adepts — these are the signs of a self-infatuated loser. He died a pathetic junkie. His evil — mostly peculiar sexual practices and bad writing — is hardly to be feared or hated.

Then what is so fascinating about the man? Likely it's simple and straightforward: he had power and power attracts. With no greatness of beauty, physical might, authority, wealth (after he'd squandered his inheritance), social capital, he still had the ability to influence and dominate others. Long dead, his presence is nonetheless still felt in the world, far more now than when he was alive.

Though never successful on the musical or theatrical stage, he had charisma, and that charisma lives on. He was a performer with the ability to utterly control an audience. His rites and ritual were on a small scale, at times private. Yet like many religious leaders, he had an overwhelming stage presence. With bizarre costumes, chants and spells, magical hand gestures, sacrifices (both real and symbolic) and special hats, he controlled others through drama.

Hakim Bey was never a follower of Crowley. The Great Beast died when the Boy-Bey was only one year old. As a young man, he recognized Crowley's influence, but wasn't pulled in by the legends of vileness and vicious behavior. Yet from the pages of *Chaos* I heard an echo, or layering of echoes, that connects the two.

Incense and crystal, dagger and sword, wand, robes, rum, cigars, candles, herbs like dried dreams — the virgin boy staring into a bowl of ink — wine and ganga, meat, yantras and gestures — rituals of pleasure, the garden of houris and sakis — the sorcerer climbs these snakes and ladders to a moment that it fully saturated with its own color.

Both magi have cult followings (most of their devotees possessing only a hazy understanding of their work.) Both traveled the world, gleaning esoteric knowledge. Both were execrated for the products of their sexual imaginations. Both saw magic as something far different than pop culture flimflam. Both knew the delights and despair associated with opium. Hakim Bey told me that he was glad that opium was still illegal in the U.S. (He'd so enjoyed his experience of it in the east that he was relieved not to be tempted by it here in America.) Both possessed the uncanny ability to make a living without having a job. (Hakim Bey let me in on the secret of *The Genghis Khan Diet For Success,* a book he never wrote: horse blood and fermented mare's milk.) Both used rites, sigils, arcane costumery, and created an air of secrecy around their work. And both had a mystique that was self-created: false names, secret societies, the alchemy of the word, and flamboyant headgear.

BIG PINK AND BOLESKINE HOUSE

I made my way, in the dark and in the cold, to Big Pink. It was December 21, the Winter Solstice, when I arrived at the spot where so much timeless music had been created. I was moved to tears, finding that place with the Yuletide shadows gathering at the end of a winding dirt road, far up in the Catskill hills. I got out and looked in the darkened windows. I'd traveled to visit Hakim Bey, but first that day, following an irrational impulse, I'd gone in search of the place where Bob Dylan and the Band had holed up a half century before, banging and wailing through a hundred lost and not-quite-found songs. For a brief while, the place was mine: total backwoods silence and solitude.

The Basement Tapes, recorded at Big Pink, are a sprawling, confused sound-hoard, and have a place in American musical mythology like few other recordings. It's a sloppy mix of folk songs, old pop tunes, gospel, country squawk, blues, and loopy originals. Exactly when individual songs were laid down will never be known. No one who was there remembers anymore, and recorded without paid engineers, with no commercial constraints, no one was writing down the facts.

Who sang on which tunes? Everybody: three, four, five voices at once sometimes. Dylan's voice is obvious, but the members of the Band blur and blend. At times though Richard Manuel's high tenor pulls free from the convivial din, coming to the front of the mix like a wave pulling out of the surf's constant motion, and breaking all by itself.

"Tears of Rage," the first track on The Band's first album, is a lament for something barely understood. There's no real rage to be heard in this song, neither in Richard's voice nor the playing of his bandmates. It's not a dirge, though it's slow and almost ceremonial. Is it a funeral or a festival we're heading toward, or both at the same time? There's certainly plenty of room for grief in the song, dream-laden and plaintive, asking over and over, "Why must I always be the thief?"

Richard keens it, a mourner at a secret rite. The first image of the song is of death and celebration, carrying a dead body "in our arms" on Independence Day. To the graveyard? To the place of patriotic speeches, fireworks, and brass bands? This is never resolved in the song, or perhaps it's just that the singer shifts focus and we lose sight of that first glimpse of heartfelt sadness and confusion.

There's also an earlier version, recorded with Dylan (who wrote the words) singing lead. This track wasn't released officially for years. But as one of the greatest songs that make up the legendary Basement Tapes, the song was stolen, bootlegged, copied, and sold under the counter and through the U.S. mail. It reached its audience like a spirit that tries to enter a house first by the door, then the windows, then comes down the chimney, a ghostly Santa Claus, through the ashes and into the place of the living.

In "Tears of Rage," I hear it all — grief, resignation, bafflement, mourning for the lost past. Time itself is the subject of the song, that endlessly disappearing world we long to inhabit (or at least gain access to for a few moments). The musical story begins at the end. It is the sound of the hidden transcendent dream-world that music can evoke for us. This isn't just a childish fantasy realm, but also the most real world there ever was and ever will be. Not the evanescence we so often take for reality, but the thing itself, in itself and of itself. The real world: rich, abundant, and true.

The two Big Pink versions are mirror images of each other. First Dylan sings lead and Richard joins with a few words on the chorus, the crying of a spirit from its ancient place of loss. But this spirit hasn't escaped from Christian hell, or drifted from the ancient Greek Hades. It's more a wailing spectral afterimage than a soul in torment for misdeeds. He's here with us, but just barely: with his impulses to despair, his austere beauty and suicidal cry.

That was what I thought I heard as I sojourned in deepening darkness from Big Pink to Woodstock, down the mountain to Hakim Bey's place. Though the ignorant tourists descended in summer swarms, looking for traces of hippie nostalgia, the famous festival had actually been held in Bethel, forty miles away. But with a long history as an arts enclave, tucked away in the Catskills, the name Woodstock stuck to the great hype-fest in the mud. And Dylan really had lived, long ago, just down the road. The village now offers yoga for yuppies, peace sign trinket shops, a dying bookstore, annoying traffic, one tolerable noodle shop, and not much else. Hakim Bey was embarrassed by the fake hippie nonsense, but he had friends in town and had found a charming house with a creek running alongside.

He'd lived ten years in South Asia, so when we went the next day to visit a Persian rug merchant, he wasn't bullshitting or showing off. In the coffee shop he sighed and shrugged when I asked about Dylan and The Band (whose pictures were displayed on the walls.) No tears of rage, just sad resignation. He was more interested in taking me to a good German butcher shop — a Metz-gerei — than in fannish rumors and faded nostalgia.

The next morning I got up early and walked the empty streets of Woodstock. In a souvenir shop window were faux-'60s pictures of the Beatles and the Rolling Stones, who'd never been near the place.

A little further on, lying in plain sight on the sidewalk was a brand new hundred dollar bill.

I felt a twinge of delight (free money!), a flicker of guilt, a moment of suspicion (was this a trick?) and then acceptance. When I showed Hakim Bey my windfall, he was delighted, proposing that we should spend it on an expensive meal in a fine restaurant. Perhaps I should have taken him out and splurged, even though such self-indulgent fare would have been wasted on me. I regret to say that the money went for gas and tolls to get me home.

It was much later that I learned what had happened the night when I sojourned to Big Pink. On that solstice, Bolskine House — the notorious haunt of Aleister Crowley, and then Jimmy Page — had been burned to the ground. Exactly as I conjured the voice of Richard Manuel out of the darkness, someone had given in to his incendiary impulses. On the farside of the Atlantic in the Scottish highlands, an anti-Crowleyite arsonist had torched the manor so long associated with satanic ritual. Winter solstice — the darkest night of year. I was far up in the Catskills, soaking in the lost echoes of music I'd once loved. Winter solstice — someone (never caught) set the demon-haunted estate to the torch. The same night, the same shadows — mad fire and tears of rage.

ANGLICAN VOODOO

When I first met Hakim Bey, his primary religious concept was Sufism. Never an orthodox Muslim, he embraced esoteric Islam's escape route from dogma, body hatred, rigidity, and rules. But his Sufism, and his enthusiasm for the Moorish Orthodox Church, flickered and faded with the years. Again and again, he'd tell me about his attraction to the church he knew as a boy. Merging various of his obsessions, he wanted to found St. Anthony of Egypt's Nonjuring Anglican Chapel of Protestant Santeria. This was one of the ever-changing names he gave to his brand of Christianity, which he proposed to magically activate. It would never become a church in the ordinary sense, yet still he had hope that it might reveal itself to be in some way real.

It wasn't the namby-pamby Saint Anthony of Padua he devoted himself to, but the wild man of the desert, Saint Anthony of Egypt, called by some the father of all hermits and religious recluses. Tempted by silver, gold, and sex demons, this early saint also attracted the devotion of visionary painters: Hieronymus Bosch, Max Ernst, and Salvador Dali. The fact that he was a cave-dweller added to his allure, along with his encounters with a genuine centaur and a satyr with a hooked snout, horns, and goat hooves.

Pan "is" Saint Anthony of Egypt, of course. We keep the outer shell of ritual beauty but read it as sheer esoteric inwardness, thus having our cake and eating it too (a fine Xtian metaphor.) All smells and bells — no theology.

Beside daydreaming of saints and private homemade rituals, one of his main practices was what he called holy parasitism — attending services at Anglican churches with good liturgy and music. He fantasized about having a few million dollars, buying a church of his own and hiring a musical director who would carry out an all-sixteenth-century-polyphany policy.

Responding to a dream I told him about, he again said that my unconscious, irrational mind had glimpsed the truth regarding his true nature. *I am in an alternate universe an Ultra High Church Anglican alcoholic reverend, leaning toward Rome, and probably de-frocked.*

A few years later, his Luddism, his loathing of recorded sound, and his love of Anglican music got tangled up, and he made a compromise.

I finally got sick of not having music in my life (a mistake, as Nietzsche said) so despite my distrust of recorded music I broke down and borrowed an I-pod, I think it's called, & arranged for a lot of mostly 16th century music to be downloaded onto it. I still can't work it very well. The trick is to LISTEN, not to use it as aural wallpaper, and when done listening to turn it off. Recordings cheapen music in a terrible way, *since the subconscious knows that it's always there when you want it, so why pay attention? Live music is yours because you're there & alive — it's a gift. Recorded music, as I've often remarked, is the tombstone of live performance. It's deathly — but then, what isn't in our charming Future post-civilization land of the hyperreal (or sub-reel) totalitarianism of the Image? Anyway, the 15-17th cen. has always been my favorite, so I've decided to "study" the period from, say, Tallis to Purcell, mostly England but also continent. Emphasis on Anglican music, which is the only kind I was ever involved in making, so I sort of "understand" it. Gee, if only the Church itself had half the intelligence & sense of beauty of its greatest music.*

PANG YANG AND PENN YAN

We found the ruins — the lost hamlet of Pang Yang — on state land between New Paltz and the Hudson River.

I was again the wheelman. Hakim Bey navigated, with maps, testimony discovered in dogged-eared books, the transcribed ramblings of a drunkard, and a quote from a tattered newspaper circa 1888. The village was almost gone, rock foundations overgrown with vines, trees crowding the ghostly hovels. Gravity had had its way, abetted by two hundred winters, grinding down the stone walls.

As we wandered there among the middens and faint outlines, hunting for grave markers, Hakim Bey smoked and murmured, reciting fragments from a poem that was taking shape in his imagination.

A tribe in the mountains . . . Tories, slaves, white, negro and Indian blood . . . the marriage of unknown and discarded . . . their language a dialect of Holland Dutch and Indian tongues . . . Mohican and Delaware . . . dugouts in the side of a hill . . . people who live in burrows as wolves and foxes . . .

swarthy as a Malay . . . piercing black eyes . . . a ghost . . . the Lady in Gray.

These gnomic utterances refer to the denizens of the almost lost outpost that we had at last found. The Lady in Gray was the spirit of their prophetess, Jemima Wilkinson, also known as the Publick Universal Friend. Ultimately settling in the Burnt Over District, she had left behind there in the Catskills a remnant of her cult. As her followers flourished, two hundred miles north and west of Pang Yang, the remaining vestiges degenerated and vanished into the earth. Some of them, rumor had it, began to practice occult arts.

It's no coincidence that the first whites to winter in my region of New York State were members of an ultraist religious group. Arriving in 1788, an advance party for the Publick Universal Friend laid the foundations of a commune that would last for more than fifty years.

And the main building — a stately, three-story manse — still stands on a hillside a few miles north of Keuka Lake. There's a historical marker out front, and a sign stating that the house is private property. The crossroads settlement of Friend and the township of Jerusalem both derive their names from this first non-Indian religious leader to settle in the Burnt-Over District.

Jemima Wilkinson, a beautiful young Quakeress, had found her religious sentiments highly aroused by the sermons of George Whitefield. Soon, a more important influence reached her and set her on the course she'd follow for life, and beyond. Much impressed by the example of Shaker leader Mother Ann Lee, Jemima's soul was highly agitated by visionary religion. She was stricken with a fever and fell into a coma. When she came back life again — in her coffin — she claimed that her original soul had died, ascended to Heaven, and her body was now inhabited by the Spirit of Life. In short, she was no longer Jemima, but a divine vessel.

Shortly, she was holding open-air meetings and gathering a coterie of passionate followers. Tall and graceful, with thick waves of dark hair and black penetrating eyes, she had no trouble bringing true believers, especially men, into her fold. With a retinue of twenty devotees, the Friend toured her native New England. She went out front on a white horse, with her robes flowing in the wind. Behind, two by two, marched the core of her new religious body.

By 1782, she had established three churches in Rhode Island and Connecticut. One of her followers was a prominent judge, who contributed a hefty sum of money and had a special annex built on his property to house the lovely vessel of God. Because of her age and beauty, rumors spread that she was using feminine, rather than divine, powers to draw men into her flock. So, like Mother Ann Lee, she declared that total celibacy was the only true godly path.

Unwelcome in her home state, driven out of Philadelphia by angry Quakers (she was even stoned at one point) she set out to establish her holy kingdom in a more receptive locale. Northward first they journeyed. In the Catskills, some of her followers stayed behind, mingled with other hill people, devolved, becoming the wild witchy folk of Pang Yang.

In 1788 the first of her adherents established themselves in the Burnt Over District, in the hills above Keuka Lake. With the substantial contributions she'd collected since her body had been claimed by God, she was able to buy 12,000 acres of prime farmland. She remained in New England until 1790, but then moved to her new seat, called Jerusalem. The wheat harvest was excellent. Soon a grist mill, a sawmill and school too were built, and at its peak — 1800 — the Friend's commune had over 250 members.

But even a vessel of God's spirit was not immune to disease. The Friend developed dropsy and the once-beautiful Jemima became bloated and deformed. She "left time" in 1819. Her successor, Rachel Malin, held a remnant of the society together until 1843. By then, dozens of the Friend's followers had deserted. Now all that remains of the commune is one surprisingly well-kept house and hundreds of people in the area with family names that had once been associated with Jerusalem.

Standing in the peaceful ruins of Pang Yang, Hakim Bey and I planned our rite of occult transmission. We agreed to set a time and a day when he would return to the ghost town and I would foray to Jerusalem. It was said that the bizarre troglodytes of Pang Yang could communicate psychically with their distant co-religionists in Penn Yan. Likewise, we agreed that we would try out this spiritual telegraph — he sending and I receiving his messages two hundred miles to the north and west.

MADNESS AND ESCAPE

Regarding lunatics, Hakim Bey admitted that he had for them a deep sympathy. Perhaps, he mused, the only thing that separated him from the mentally ill was the act of writing. He called this gift Schizopoesis.

I told him about visiting a friend in a locked psych ward of Rochester's largest hospital. The elevator door opened and a guy got on from the floor where they did electro-convulsive therapy. He was eating a stick of homemade jerked meat of indeterminate origin. He asked, "Want some?" Completely out of character (being germphobic and not normally friendly with meat-wielding strangers) I took a bite. That day, and the next, I waited, expecting dire medical consequences. But apparently I'd been under the protection of St. Dymphna (patroness of the mentally afflicted) or some unknown pagan deity. No illness, nor even digestive discomfort, followed.

The next letter from Hakim Bey began with this: "Don't take meat from strangers," – didn't you hear that over and over when you were little? Tsk.

He continued with this rumination on madness and distraction.

I've "just" realized that writing poetry and studying Hermeticism is like being constantly on a sort of subliminal dose (say 50 mics) of LSD – giving rise to s(t)imulations of ESP-like sensitivity to psychic environment – fine when one is writing, or contemplating Nature, but not fine in NYC, or even Main St. in New Paltz, or trying to deal with lawyers or bankers. I guess this is "flashback," or that we all did in fact suffer Permanent Brain Damage in the 60s (we considered P.B.D. a term of high praise) and of course my current herbal self-medication only adds to the effect, I'm sure. But I believe many people – perhaps nearly all – have the same experience but repress it with distractions, noise, job, chitchat, prozac, etc. till they become numb enough to function. (Even now, as if to puncture this thought, the sound of electric guitars comes from somewhere – I turn on a fan to drown it out.)

In sufism you're supposed to be able to deal with this and not succumb to astral oppression or disgust with "the World" – not run off to rural monastaries like Christians and Buddhists. Maybe this works in a pre-technopathocratic culture? In India, they expected people my age to go off and live in a forest ashram and meditate. In our culture we're expected to go into a hospital and pay for it. People consume media in self-defense against "too much reality." This is one of the things I use books for: escape. For me TV dulls the imagination and is actually a failure as a distraction (I've always called it 5th rate heroin.) The computer is twice, maybe 10 times worse. But books, art, live music and performance stimulate *and arouse imagination (or are meant to, if they succeed) – this kind of "escapism" is necessary, what Nietzsche called Will to Power as Art. (Escapism = Resistance.) Of course what I'm saying (in prose) is too crude. The spirit bloweth where it listeth, even (once in a while) in pop culture.*

Then the letter describes various projects (including a new Moorish Orthodox Ashram and Retreat), a play he's writing (which takes place on the moon – somewhat influenced by Thorne Smith's *Night Life of the Gods,* but in poetry and much dirtier) and another Irish writer I'd never heard of, but who I must track down and read. He closes with: *Well – don't take any wooden jerky.*

THE HIDDEN

Digging through my stacks of letters (which are only in approximate order, as he never dated them) I found a 3 by 5 printed card. On it is this poem:
I want to tell you of my love
But can find no Hidden place to do it in —
Or, if I find the place, my rival is there ahead.
Or, if at last I find a place
And you there alone,
Alas! It is myself who is lost now —
I faded away entire.
Anon.
Find a Hidden Place – the Moorish Orthodox Church

I called, reaching across the miles and years, and asked him about this bit of yellowing ephemera.

It's from the '60s. We gave them away.

And who wrote it?

A moment of honesty and clarity. *I don't know. It might have been me. I don't remember.*

Like the passports issued by Noble Drew Ali, like the diploma I was granted, establishing the Ziggurat Lodge in the Burnt Over District, this card has power beyond mere ink and paper. The MOC did not prostelytize. It ensorcelled, enchanted, seduced.

This sent me searching in my attic, in the Scriptorium, as certain of my more enlightened friends call it. Behind a framed photo of a young, hyper-hip Miles Davis, I found the item I had hoped still existed.

On a shelf in the lower chamber of his Wallkill River retreat, beside his photo of King Farouk, there had been an amulet about 4 inches tall and 6 inches wide. The word "Al-Batin" stood out in graceful Arabic script. The background was a faint, gently-writhing web of tendrils. Below the Arabic characters was the meaning in English. Al-Batin is The Hidden.

My memory is still quite good, but that is not the reason I recall this amulet so well. On one of my visits, long ago, I took the obscure object to a stationery store in New Paltz and made a copy. I glued my black and white facsimile on stiff backing and displayed it on my office wall for years. It had disappeared, but now (conjured by a far-off voice) it had returned from occultation.

Again on the phone, I asked about the amulet. That night, I got another hint that he was beginning to fade from the world. His letters had become infrequent and his handwriting – once beautiful - had gotten shaky. In one he asked, *Why can't I mellow out in my dotage and become a Rich Buddhist like everyone else?*

Regarding the Al-Batin amulet, he said, simply and humbly, that he didn't remember it.

This is disturbing to hear, yet also perfect for such an item. Al-Batin (which also means "the inner" or "the inward") is one of the 99 Most Beautiful Names of Allah: the divine as the Hidden One who can not be seen but exists in every realm. It indicates an occult meaning, the reality behind apparent forms. Some Sufis say that every person has a batin in the world of souls, the self cleansed by spiritual light.

He did not remember the amulet anymore. It exists now only for me: my facsimile set up on the table where I write these words. My memory, my possession, revealed now, soon to be returned to its Hidden Place. Alongside that I have placed The Hidden Card.

Alas! It is myself who is lost now –
I faded away entire.

BACK TO THE CAVES

Translated into two dozen languages, Hakim Bey's influence extends its thousand tentacles and caressing ectoplasmic fingers. No matter how hard scholars or archivists labor, they will never capture his essence. No one will ever create a bibliography that entirely encompasses his true work. There are items in my archive — letters, poems, a few squares of gold leaf — no one else has ever seen. Likewise, others possess bits and pieces, charmed fragments and lost arcana.

The personage called "Hakim Bey" was slipping away into the shadows whence he came. Like Houdini and the Count of Monte Cristo, he had long dreamed of escape – to wriggle out, fade away into the underbrush, head for the hills, vanish. Disappearance, he declares in *Black Fez Manifesto*, is a very logical radical option for our time, not at all a disaster or death.

To vanish is not to plunge into nonexistence; it is an act that reclaims one's freedom. To achieve true ontological obscurity, to be a "Long Gone Daddy," as Hank Williams would say, is to achieve a kind of triumph. B. Traven, who wrote *The Treasure of the Sierra Madre* and other anti-capitalist adventures, is a hero of disappearance. (Even his real name has never been established.) Rimbaud is another, his entire poetical work finished before he was twenty and vanished into obscurity. And Jim Wheat – the most brilliant, twistedly clever humorist I've ever read — what happened to him? No one seems to know.

In occultation (literally: to be hidden from view or lost to notice) true freedom can sometimes be found. Failure is *the last possible outside.* In lost-and-not-found landscapes the marvelous and free can still flourish. In his oblique and opaque way, Hakim Bey pointed to a blasted heath, a new dust bowl, and vast garbage dumps, as failure-zones in which possibility lies dormant.

Places of failure and abandonment do not mean, however, mere disaster areas. In some ways, even these have a celebrity and glamor. Consider the fame of Love Canal, America's premier toxic waste suburban hell-zone (which I've visited more than once). Chernobyl, Fukushima, Dresden and the Pine Barrens of New Jersey too have their attraction, a lore and allure. Instead of that, Hakim Bey proposed a connoisseurship of the unspectacular, the poor and sad, far more plausible in the forgotten, ignored, lost, abandoned places without the romance of catastrophe.

In a letter, he went further: *The exception might be found in what the alchemists call the "dung heap" – utterly despised as having no price – dreck that no one will pay for, like self-published poetry or handmade Xmas cards or idle chat in a park on a summer day. I like the idea of art that leaves no trace – buried burnt sunk dismantled and or eaten.*

In *Black Fez Manifesto*, he calls for endarkenment and poetic vandalism. The book also includes texts of The Cro-Magnon Liberation Front. Their slogan: Back to the Caves! He dreams of ruined factories and ritual sledgehammers, claiming that Thoreau was Cro-Magnon when he visualized ragweed and mushrooms pushing up through asphalt and concrete.

The Cro-Magnons are long gone, though their genes continue in some of us. Living in a cave – like Saint Anthony of Egpyt, an Indian guru, a bear, or ancient human – has little attraction for me. The isolation is a draw, but I'm too spoiled by comfort to even fantasize about such a retreat from the modern world. Still, to escape inward, if not physically then into the caverns of my own skull, is perhaps a doorway to the Last Outside,

Grand metaphysical failure and the ordinary failings of the human form seem only distantly related. But biological failure, as in the Cro-Magnon's disappearance from the planet, offers some appeal, if not hope. I'm reminded of the Voluntary Human Extinction Movement ("Live Long and Die Out") and the Church of Euthanasia. To some, the real Hakim Bey was just an old hippie with health problems, many friends, and profound sadness. Getting old was much worse than he feared. Work was the only pleasure the doctors didn't forbid him. Though no writer who has reached a large and avid audience can be said to have failed, the human body ultimately shows us all how limited our efforts must be.

I keep waiting for bad news just praying that my fate can be put off a while longer. The future is shit. We know that. Occasionally & perversely the present can prove otherwise for a moment. In the last few years I've come to feel that only escapism makes sense vis-à-vis a society given over to hitherto-unimaginable idiocy, bad taste, and cruelty. Hence my retreat (to the country, to poetry, etc.) & increasing disengagement from everything else. My only question now is: have I retreated far enough? Am I invisible yet?

America became increasingly horrible for him to contemplate. He went to look for the Devil's Danskammer (where Indians held great ritual dances – a rock jutting over the Hudson River north of Newburgh) and found it transformed into Dynergy Corp. – a totally sinister huge power plant with chainlink fences and armed guards. This somehow seemed exactly right, as a symbol of the Approaching End.

As the years passed, he became more disgusted and depressed by the smug cheesy plastic alienation and hopeless boredom he saw all around him. He began investigating ways of escaping America again, to Ireland, Canada, Holland. But he admitted that he was too old to start over again in a new country.

Failure may even be a sign of election – of paradoxical success from the very Abyss. Every moment snatched from the Hegelian Absolute Free Market infinite shopping mall of the Police State is Paradise Now.

As the end neared, he went back to his deepest love. *In one sense the decision to return to poetry was anti-formalistic in that I got tired of trying to make sense and of defending myself with scholarship. Geez, I mean, who's keeping score?? I feel a liberating exhilaration, released from constraints (self-imposed) of authorial responsibility.*

Years back, Hakim Bey had encouraged me to stay irrational. Today, I still hold this advice close to my heart. Going in to get out — the involution of thought and imagination — may indeed be the only way to reach what he called the Last Outside. With all this vanishing and escape, it's no coincidence that when *Temporary Autonomous Zone* was published, the original subtitle ("the pleasures of disappearance") had disappeared.

If Hakim Bey was a figment of his own imagination – a specter called out of his own dreaming — if he existed only in books and recordings — wafting through the aether in radio waves and spieling away one to one with me — words, words, and more words — if Hakim Bey could travel in his mind through the astral planes, then it doesn't matter that his earthly form is now lifeless. He was a ghost when still alive, so how much different is it now that the tired, sick, old man which contained his spectral multitudes is no more?

Riding the earth around the sun for seventy some years had the usual effect. In the end, the banal weakness of the human body triumphed, as it does for all of us. Hakim Bey never claimed or longed for fame, but he did achieve temporary immortality – which, he said, is certainly better than none at all.

PENN YAN AND PANG YANG

I drove deep into the Burnt Over District, to Penn Yan, where the Publik Universal Friend had established her cult, lived out her last years, and then left time. Keuka Lake is Y-shaped, and Penn Yan is a small town at the tip of the eastern fork. In the heart of the Finger Lakes, vineyards here occupy much of the landscape, warmed by the lakes and sheltered by the rise and fall of hillsides. As a boy, I'd been to Penn Yan a number of times. My father had bought twenty-five acres (much of it abandoned vineyards which he tried to restore) on the V-shaped bluff formed by Keuka's two prongs.

The standard story of how Penn Yan got its name is a muddle of conjecture and falsehood. Pennsylvanians and New England Yankees converged here in some imaginary conclave. Until I met Hakim Bey, I hadn't given the name much thought. My family had long before sold the land and I'd only been through the town a few times since, on the way to some other burnt over location.

But walking with Hakim Bey in the ruins of Pang Yang in the Hudson Valley, listening to his musings about mixed-blood hill people and the strange tongues they spoke, talking with him about the Lady in Gray and rumors of telepathic communication between the two villages, I understood that Penn Yan was far more than a quaint little tourist town.

After Hakim Bey had left time, I returned to Penn Yan in a heightened state of perception. That is, I was hoping that some message might travel across the miles and years, across the border between life and death.

Over the decades, we had talked about him coming to visit me in the Burnt Over District. Buses and trains could easily have brought him here, but he never made the journey in the flesh. I wanted to show him my favorite sites: the Church of the Hypercube, the Mormon high holyland, Spiritualist shrines, the Lovecraft stained glass window at the church where he could have basked in candlelit Anglican Voodoo music. I proposed that he come to Rochester via public transport, we'd soak up occult power at the sites here, then we could drive back to the Hudson Valley together, visiting the Cardiff Giant, the village of Stone Arabia, and the Oneida Perfectionist commune on our way.

By the time I'd offered this plan however, travel had become an intolerable burden for him. He'd sojourned for ten years in India and Iran, and later been flown to Ireland, Slovenia, and Holland by devotees of the TAZ. But a six hour train trip would have been – in the last few years – too much. So he never walked the mantic soil (to use his words) of the Burnt Over District.

The landscape itself is mantic: hills, river, canal, lakes having the power of divination. That power, however, had to be activated, conjured out of its long haunted sleep.

On the last day of August, as the summer was dying, I drove into the countryside and arrived in Penn Yan. The thunder clouds and rain held back for as long as I wandered there. On the side of the Birkett Mills building hung a twenty-eight foot wide griddle, which had once been used to make the biggest pancake in the world. At the other end of the breakfast spectrum was a diner that made a U-boat's galley seem spacious. I'm not tall and I could easily touch the ceiling. Everything, except the overfed custumors, was miniature, packed in tightly. I have no love of Disney's dynasty, yet I expected and perhaps hoped for a glimpse of seven dwarves scuttling around in the cramped and steamy kitchen. Next door was – no surpise — the Masonic lodge, and across the street I found a historical marker informing me this was the location of the Owl's Nest Hotel, "which stood along a boat basin."

My sojourn ended at the water's edge. A stretch of grass and trees provided a cordon between the town proper and the shore of Keuka Lake. I had the place to myself. On a sunny day, the little park would have been filled with noise, noxious picnic odors, and commotion. On this day, a vast lead gray expanse stretched overhead, with not a glimpse of blue to be seen. And not a single boat marred the lake's peace. Somewhere, near but invisible, gulls and crows cast up their lonesome cries. Closer, I heard crickets and the lapping of the wavelets on the shore. A lone duck, the aetheric double of the one which had appeared on Hakim Bey's postage stamp thirty-seven years before, made quickly-disappearing circles in the lake's surface.

I hadn't come expecting great revelation. My purpose was to open a channel between Pang Yang and Penn Yan, between Hakim Bey (no longer of the earth) and myself. His first words to me came back. *We want to be amazed.* In the resurrected *Monitor* he'd declared, *We want sacred madness.* He'd told me once that consciousness must *reverberate and expand like waves or spirals or music.*

I'd listened to Dervish music that morning, as I drove past fields of corn and hay. And coming into Penn Yan, I'd played the original version of Dylan's "Knockin' On Heaven's Door." Yes, a long black cloud was coming down. Now, thunder rolled over the lake, over the bluff on the far side, over the whole of the Burnt Over District.

I'd brought a sprig of native tobacco, grown by a Buddhist friend for ritual uses. Standing on the shore, I lit a match and got the tobacco burning. The scent was far sweeter than the cigarettes and cannabis that Hakim Bey smoked. Grown in mantic soil, the plant released the power of divination. I closed my eyes and inhaled deeply.

Soon, the leaves and buds were ash, but the scent remained. And with that scent – out of the earth and out of the past – came a voice. It wasn't a literal sound that others might have heard, but it was clear and distinctive: Hakim Bey saying my name. Perhaps it was a just memory of hearing him on the phone. Perhaps it was – to use one of his favorite words – imaginal. Nonetheless, I heard it, his voice reaching me from far away.

As long as the scent lingered, I stood there on the shore, not clinging to the sound in my head, but holding onto what I'd lost and what I'd found. I was not amazed that day, nor taken by sacred madness. But my consciousness did indeed reverberate and expand. Waves on the lake's surface. Spirals of grief and gratitude. And a voice, making music out of words.

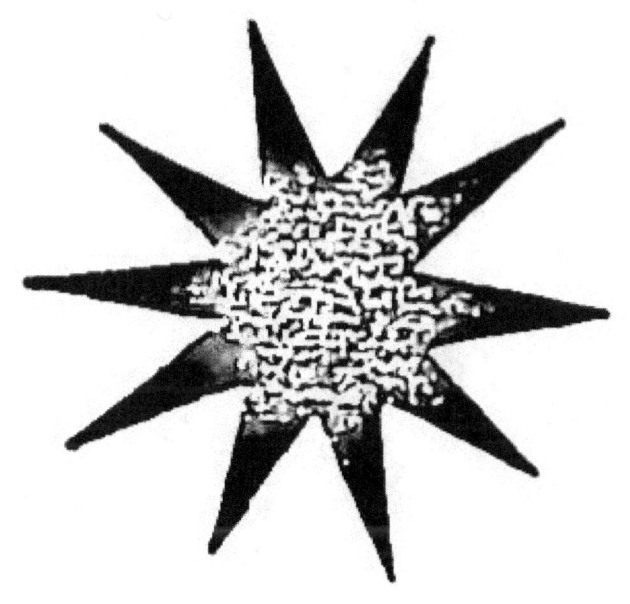

"Be the first
on your horizon
to be greeted!"

PLW / HB
SELECT BIBLIOGRAPHY

by Trevor Blake

I first crossed paths with Hakim Bey in the same way as Th. Metzger, through a solicitation to contribute to *semiotext(e) USA*. Bey and I had a regular exchange through the mail. My zine *OVO* was the first to publish some of the essays that were later collected in *TAZ*. It was Hakim Bey who introduced me to Th. Metzger.

I first met Hakim Bey in person in New York City, at an anarchist bookstore. He invited me go to the office of Autonomedia, to help in the production of *semiotext(e) USA*. The printer had refused to print four pages of the book. Autonomedia had found a second printer willing to print just those four pages. The forbidden folio was folded, stuffed in an envelope and affixed to the inside back cover of *semiotext(e) USA*, rendering the book whole.

I folded and stuffed with Bey and with another out-of-town guest, P. M., author of *bolo'bolo*. Our labor was compensated by a fine pasta dinner. I asked P. M. to sign *bolo'bolo* for me. He was confused, and said "You know, no one knows I have written this book, not my family or friends, I have never signed a copy, this will be the first." And then he signed it.

The next day Bey was not available, but Peter Wilson and I and a few others met for lunch. Peter and I talked about intellectual property. He said he kept it simple. Books by Bey were in the public domain and anyone could do anything they wanted with them, while works by Wilson were subject to copyright "and they'd better pay... or at least ask."

I kept in touch with Hakim Bey in person, on the telephone and through the mail until he spoke no more. Th. Metzger knew him better than me and better than most. Only he could draw this curtain.

There are hundreds of essays, journals, zines, handbills, flyers, posters and other ephemera attributed to Bey and Wilson, and perhaps hundreds more that went unattributed. Let them find you.

Abecedarium. West Lima: Xexoxial Editions, 2010.

Aimless Wanderings: Chuang Tzu's Chaos Linguistics. La Farge: Xexoxial, 2015.

Akashic Record of the Astral Convention, 1987.

American Revolution as a Gigantic Real Estate Scam, The. New York: Autonomedia, 2019.

Angels. New York: Pantheon Books, 1980.

Atlantis Manifesto. Woodstock: Shivastan, 2003.

Avant Gardening: Ecological Struggle in the City & the World (with Bill Weinberg). New York: Autonomedia, 1999.

Ayahuasca and Shamanism (with Michael Taussig). New York: Autonomedia, 2002.

Between Dog & Wolf (with David Levi Strauss). Brooklyn: Autonomedia, 2010.

Black Fez Manifesto. New York: Autonomedia, 2008.

Carnival. 1985.

Chaos: The Broadsheets of Ontological Anarchism. Weehawken: Grim Reaper Books, 1985.

Christian Poem for the Late Ira Cohen, A. Woodstock: Shivastan Press, 2016.

Cross-Dressing in the Anti-Rent War: With Poems for Occasions, Egyptian Sonnets, and Ghazals & Letters. Portable Press at Yo-Yo Labs, 2006.

Dimensions Expanded Explored (anthology). Otterlo: Rijksmuseum Kröller-Müller, 1992.

Divine Flashes (anthology). London: SPCK, 1982.

Drunken Universe, The (with Nasr Purjavadi). New Lebanon: Omega, 1999.

Ec(o)logues. Barrytown: Station Hill, 2014.

Ecstatic Incisions (with Freddie Baer). Stirling: AK Press 1992.

Escape From the Nineteenth Century. New York: Autonomedia, 1998.

False Documents. Barrytown: Station Hill, (n.d.).

False Messiah: Crypto-Xtian Tracts & Fragments. New York: Autonomedia, 2022.

Forget the Kaaba: Verse & Translations. Teheran, 1977.

Forty Poems from the Divan (with Nasiri Khusraw). Tehran: Imperial Iranian Academy of Philosophy, 1977.

Gone to Croatan (anthology). New York: Autonomedia, 1993.

Green Hermeticism: Alchemy & Ecology (anthology). Great Barrington: Lindisfarne Books, 2007.

Heart's Witness (anthology). Tehran: Imperial Iranian Academy of Philosophy, 1978.

Heresies: Anarchist Memoirs, Anarchist Art. New York: Autonomedia, 2016.

Hoodoo Metaphysics. Brooklyn: Bearpuff Press, 2019.

Immediatism. AK Press, San Francisco, 1994.

Interzone (anthology). London: Simon & Schuster, 1988.

Long 1980s, The (Nick Aikens, editor). Amsterdam: Valiz, 2018.

Mask (anthology). Aspen: Baldwin Gallery, 2005.

Millennium. Brooklyn: Autonomedia, 1996.

Mohawk Anglican Freemasons. Hudson: Publication Studio, 2020.

Nostalgia / Utopia. Munich: Hirmer Verlag, 2012.

Old Calendrists, The. Enemy Combatant Publications, 2016.

Orgies of the Hemp Eaters. New York: Autonomedia, 2004.

Opium Dens I Have Known. Woodstock: Shivastan Press, 2014.

Outlaw Bible of American Poetry, The (anthology). New York: Thunder's Mouth Press 1999.

Peacock Angel: the Esoteric Tradition of the Yezidis. Rochester: Inner Traditions, 2022.

Pirate Utopias. New York: Autonomedia, 1995.

Ploughing the Clouds: the Search for Irish Soma. San Francisco: City Lights Books, 1999.

Radio Sermonettes. New York: Libertarian Book Club, 1992.

Rain Queer. Boulder: Farfalla Press, 2009.

Sacred Drift: Essays on the Margins of Islam. San Francisco: City Lights Books, 1993.

Saqqakhaneh (anthology). Tehran: Museum of Contemporary Art, (n.d.)

Scandal: Essays in Islamic Heresy. New York: 1988, 1988.

School of Nite. New York: Spuyten Duyvil, 2016.

Search for Sodom and Gomorrah (with Jacob Rabinowitz). Kansas City: Acme Safe Co., 1963.

semiotex(e) Polysexuality New York: Autonomedia, 1981.

semiotex(e) SF. New York: Autonomedia, 1989.

semiotex(e) USA 13. New York: Autonomedia, 1987.

Shower of Stars. New York: Autonomedia, 1996.

Spiritual Destinations of an Anarchist. New York: Autonomedia, 2015.

Spiritual Journeys of an Anarchist. New York: Autonomedia, 2014.

Storm, The. Edited by Mark A. Sullivan. New York, 1976.

T.A.Z.: the Temporary Autonomous Zone, Ontological Anarchy, Poetic Terrorism. New York: Autonomedia, 1991.

Technoscience and Cyberculture (anthology). New York: Routledge, 1996.

Temple of Perseus at Panopolis, The. New York: Autonomedia, 2017.

Traditional Modes of Contemplation and Action. Tehran: Imperial Iranian Academy of Philosophy, 1977.

Un coup d'état nietzschéen (with Hervé Denès, Jackie Reuss). Montreuil: L'Insomniaque, 2014.

Unbearables (anthology). New York: Autonomedia, 1995.

Utopian Trace. Asheville: Logosophia, 2019.

Vanished Signs. Hudson: Lunar Chandelier, 2018.

Weaver of Tales (with Karl Schlamminger). München: Callwey Verlag, 1980.

Winter Calligraphy of Ustad Selim, & Other Poems, The. Ipswich: Golgonooza Press, 1975.

TH. METZGER
SELECT BIBLIOGRAPHY

Beautiful City of the Dead (as Leander Watts). New York: Houghton Mifflin, 2006.

Beware, the Invisible Hellhole! Rochester: Th. Metzger, 1988.

Big Gurl (with Richard P. Scott). New York: New American Library, 1989.

Big Noise on the Astral Plane. Rochester: Ziggurat, 2021.

Birth of Heroin and the Demonization of the Dope Fiend, The. Port Townsend: Breakout Productions, 1998.

Blood and Volts. Brooklyn: Autonomedia, 1996.

Devil in a Dead Man's Underwear. Rochester: Ziggurat, 1993.

Do the Do. Rochester: Th. Metzger, 1989.

Drowning in Fire. New York: Signet Books, 1992.

Flaherty's Wake: Abortionist, Lawyer, Boxer, Priest. Rochester: Ziggurat 2023.

Hydrogen Sleep and Speed. Providence: The Poet's Press, 2011.

Meet Me in the Strange (as Leander Watts). Atlanta: Meercat Press, 2018.

Select Strange and Sacred Sites. Brooklyn: Autonomedia, 2002.

Send Now for Your Satano-Miraculous Oozejob! Rochester: Ziggurat, 1998.

Shock Totem. New York: Penguin Books, 1991.

St. Vibrissa, Virgin, Martyr, & Stigmatrix. Rochester: Th. Metzger, 1988.

Stonecutter (as Leander Watts). New York: Houghton Mifflin, 2002.

Ten Thousand Charms (as Leander Watts). New York: Houghton Mifflin, 2005.

This is Your Final Warning! Brooklyn: Autonomedia, 1992.

Tweye Poems. Buffalo: Raccoon Books, 1985.

Undercover Mormon: a Spy in the House of the Gods. Southbury: Roadswell Editions, 2012.

Wild Ride to Heaven (as Leander Watts). New York: Houghton Mifflin, 2003.

mogtus-sanlux

publisher

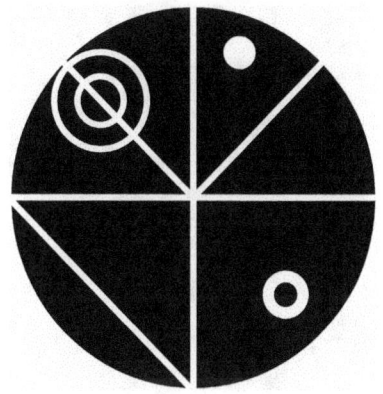

"A procession of the damned. By the damned, I mean the excluded. We shall have a procession of data that Science has excluded. Battalions of the accursed, captained by pallid data that I have exhumed, will march. You'll read them — or they'll march. Some of them livid and some of them fiery and some of them rotten."

Charles Fort
The Book of the Damned

Public catalog: mogtus-sanlux.one
Private catalog: ~mogtus-sanlux